Waterfalls of New Brunswick: A Guide
2nd Edition

Also by NICHOLAS GUITARD:

The Lost Wilderness: Rediscovering W.F. Ganong's New Brunswick
Waterfalls of New Brunswick: A Guide (1st edition)
Waterfalls of New Brunswick

Waterfalls
of New Brunswick
A GUIDE 2nd EDITION

NICHOLAS GUITARD

Edited by Alison Hughes.
Cover and page design by Julie Scriver.
Cover and interior photographs by Nicholas Guitard unless otherwise noted.
Cover images: Roger Brook Falls (front) and Hells Kitchen Falls (back).
Maps by Todd Graphic, toddgraphic.ns.ca.
Printed in China by MCRL Overseas Group.
10 9 8 7 6 5 4 3 2 1

Library and Archives Canada Cataloguing in Publication

Title: Waterfalls of New Brunswick : a guide / Nicholas Guitard.
Names: Guitard, Nicholas, 1956- author.
Description: 2nd edition.
Identifiers: Canadiana 20200311239 | ISBN 9781773101859 (softcover)
Subjects: LCSH: Waterfalls—New Brunswick— Guidebooks. | LCSH: Trails—New Brunswick— Guidebooks. | LCSH: New Brunswick—Guidebooks.
Classification: LCC GB1430.N5 G85 2021 | DDC 551.48/4097151—dc23

Goose Lane Editions is located on the traditional unceded territory of the Wəlastəkwiyik whose ancestors along with the Mi'kmaq and Peskotomuhkati Nations signed Peace and Friendship Treaties with the British Crown in the 1700s.

Goose Lane Editions acknowledges the generous financial support of the Government of Canada, the Canada Council for the Arts, and the Province of New Brunswick.

Goose Lane Editions
500 Beaverbrook Court, Suite 330
Fredericton, New Brunswick
CANADA E3B 5X4
gooselane.com

To my wife Belinda, for your encouragement, kindness, and – most of all – your unwavering love.

81. Hermit Falls (bonus fall)

Contents

90. Lamb Falls (bonus fall)

Preface

Over the past few years, the notion of revising my original waterfall guide had crossed my mind. Then, like most people, I experienced life events that redirected my attention or was just lulled into a state of procrastination, and ideas – such as rewriting a guide – floated past much like water over a waterfall. At the urging and support of my wife, Belinda, and the folks at Goose Lane Editions, and of course the encouragement of waterfall enthusiasts, I decided to pull myself out of my self-induced funk and get my hiking boots dirty once more.

Prior to the 2010 publication of *Waterfalls of New Brunswick*, scarcely any information on the topic of waterfalls existed in our province. Since then, to my delight, this has changed. All anyone has to do is start a Google search of the topic, and numerous sites and Facebook pages will appear. I must say the quality of the photography and information found on the internet is superb. I feel gratified with the increased uptake of my original guide by people who want to search for and visit waterfalls, as well as get to know our province a wee bit better. I have always maintained that we are not a drive-through province but Canada's Picture Province.

During public presentations about my books, people have commented positively on the waterfall guide. Once, a couple approached and thanked me for saving their marriage, while other folks have credited the book with giving their lives a sense of purpose. While visiting waterfalls with family and friends, I meet enthusiasts who ask to have their copies of the guide signed. On one occasion, I met a grandmother and her two grandsons at the Starkey covered bridge at the mouth of Long Creek. During the conversation, I noticed her tattered guide on the passenger seat next to her, held together with duct tape. We had a wonderful discourse about the guide as I autographed her copy.

While leafing through her guide, noticing all the check marks and notes, I realized how much people appreciated my effort in writing it. The first waterfall guide gave me the opportunity to establish new friendships. Through these friendships, I have had ample opportunity to explore and photograph many exceptional locations in our picture province. One of the things I have enjoyed the most has been travelling around the province to municipal libraries to give presentations and share our common enthusiasm. It was extra special when I was asked on numerous occasions to present my photographs and narratives about my waterfall excursions to school students. I always made an effort to encourage youngsters' interest in discovering New Brunswick.

The original guide was not without detractors. It was suggested by some that, if and when a second version were to be issued, the waterfalls located on or near their properties be omitted. Others asked for improved driving directions and maps that include trails, and still others asked for more colour images.

With that said, what has changed with this latest guide to New Brunswick waterfalls? To start, I have adopted the new format used by the publisher for all of their outdoor guides. It makes for a larger guide with all colour images and detailed coloured maps with roads, hiking routes, and waypoints for the trailheads and waterfalls indicated. I believe this enhances the guide's usability. As well, I decided to replace approximately sixty of the original waterfalls with others that I believe fit the needs of all types of enthusiast. It should be noted that I attempted to include waterfalls from as many New Brunswick counties as possible.

The photographs for this guide were taken over a period of ten years, and I made a concerted effort to capture images of waterfalls that render their natural splendour. Searching through my archives of images, though, it was sometimes difficult to select pictures that portrayed a sense of how I felt while enjoying the natural serenity of a particular waterfall. For several waterfalls, a return visit was required. Unfortunately, the summer of 2020 will be remembered for its lack of rain and, of course, the COVID-19 pandemic, which changed and hindered my plans for a return.

There have been physical changes to the waterfalls, as well as to the guide. A good example is Walton Glen Gorge. Plenty has changed since my first visit there in 2007. At that time, very few people made the trip to the gorge and fewer trekked through the Eye of the Needle. As I type, the Fundy Parkway has been extended to include Walton Glen with improved hiking pathways, a lookout platform, and improved access to the Eye of the Needle. Change is inevitable, especially in a province dependent upon forestry to drive the economy. In this regard, some trails and access roads will change between the writing and sale of this new guide.

I am sure you will appreciate this updated version of the guide. So, I urge you to get your hiking boots on, and let's hope our paths cross on the trails to the waterfalls of New Brunswick.

Introduction

I will begin by apologizing to those enthusiasts who submitted suggestions if I have omitted their favourite waterfalls. Thank you for your interest. Unfortunately, timelines were tight and the quantity too large. As I sit here typing, the names of numerous waterfalls that I wish I could have included are rambling through my mind. With that said, this guide features the information necessary to visit over one hundred New Brunswick waterfalls (including the bonus falls listed at the end of some entries). The intent of this updated guide is to provide a level of waterfalling adventure for a broad spectrum of enthusiasts. It provides information that will help users with mobility issues to visit waterfalls and contains details that will challenge those interested in further adventure. To this end, there are waterfalls that can be seen from a car by simply pulling off to one side of the highway, such as Little Lepreau River Falls in Saint John County. There are others that are reached by a short hike on an established trail, such as Falls Brook Falls in Madawaska County, and still others requiring a strenuous hike with steep ascents and bushwhacking through the wilderness, such as the waterfall on the East Branch Point Wolfe River in Albert County.

To encourage day trips in our province, the waterfalls listed in the guide follow the New Brunswick Department of Tourism and Parks Scenic Drives. Our province features a wide variety of waterfall types, resulting from differences in the ways in which they were formed. The guide is structured to make each waterfall experience as enjoyable as possible. At the beginning of each waterfall, I've included useful information such as the closest community, the county, an associated watercourse, and map names and numbers, as well as a quick reference for the difficulty of the hike. The most important feature is the waterfall GPS coordinates. Each coordinate has been tested to ensure correctness. To know what to expect with each trip, I have added simple classifications to each waterfall description and listed them to provide a quick summary of what the trip entails. Each of these classifications is clarified in the following description. Whether you are an avid outdoorsperson wanting a challenge or a family looking for a nice location to visit, New Brunswick has a waterfall waiting for you.

Beyond the beauty of the waterfalls are the stories. Every chance meeting with people or animals, and each mishap along the way, are forever part of your story. The appeal of waterfalling goes well beyond the hike. The waterfall is the reward at the end of your hike, oftentimes after the added adventure of bushwhacking through thick forest or scrambling down into a ravine, that makes it worthwhile.

Venturing out into the countryside is the best way to appreciate our numerous waterfalls. Exploring these significant areas, we encounter nature on its own terms; we also make a journey of self-discovery through our personal connection with the natural world.

Our attraction to waterfalls is deeply rooted in our curiosity about water in motion, its constant and relentless change. It is rooted in our desire for self-discovery. Taking the path less journeyed – from wild spring torrents to summer trickles, from bright autumn colours to spectacular winter ice sculptures – our waterfalls will not disappoint.

The following information on how to use the guide will enhance user enjoyment and facilitate a better exploration of each waterfall. It is essential to note that some of the material is based on my personal experience in the woods and my research into each waterfall.

Waterfall name: The verification of the name of each waterfall was made using various sources. From the earliest documented history of the Wolastoqey and Mi'kmaq Nations, river systems have been essential to existence and are part of the New Brunswick story. For example, the place name Shogomoc has several meanings in Wolastoqey, but the most predominately used one is derived from seeogamook, meaning "place of chiefs." During the period of European settlement, many of the rivers and, in some cases, waterfalls such as Sproul Settlement Falls, were renamed by families that homesteaded in the area. Names such as Hells Kitchen and Match Factory Falls were given to denote a location where log drives were dangerous or a life-changing event occurred.

Many of the locations in the guide have official names that can be found in Alan Rayburn's *Geographical Names of New Brunswick* (1975) or on the Natural Resources Canada site for searching geographical names at http://www4.rncan .gc.ca/search-place-names/search?lang=en. Yet, there are many locations that are not on any official list but are known locally by names such as Trickle Falls or Split Rock Falls. Regardless of the source, this guide utilizes the most commonly known name. Not unique to New Brunswick is another practice of naming watercourses to depict a particular quality of the river on a regional basis. As a result, there are many waterfalls with similar names and many known by default as Falls Brook Fall, Rocky Brook Fall, or Trout Brook Fall. In fact, there are at least four locations known as Fall(s) Brook Falls in Restigouche County alone. Where the waterfall had no descriptive name, it was named after the source of the water, such as Gagne Brook Falls. This naming quirkiness is genuine and part of our heritage.

Type: The types of waterfall are mainly based on the geological reasons for their formation. By overlaying our river systems on a geological map of New Brunswick, or for that matter on a topographical map, the relative locations and the reasons for the different types become evident. Waterfalls are also formed by various phenomena beyond geology. Although the majority are at geological transition points, glaciers and the glacial debris that remained are other contributing factors.

There are numerous adjectives to describe a type of waterfall. In some cases, the reason for the description is apparent: for example, the fan shape of Welsford Falls. Many waterfalls are a combination of types, and the description that fits best was chosen. To maintain consistency throughout the region, this guide follows the type names used by Benoit Lalonde in his beautiful *Waterfalls in Nova Scotia*. You can expect to find the following:

Cascade: A waterfall that drops in elevation in a series of small steps.

Drop: A fall where the watercourse drops over the edge without contacting the rock face, sometimes making a space to walk behind the waterfall.

Fan: A fall that erupts over the edge through a narrow channel and widens out across the rock face.

Slide: A fall similar to a cascade except the water remains in contact with the bedrock throughout and does not have any steps.

Tiered: A fall with distinct drops over multiple levels that may or may not change the direction of the water.

Height: There was no attempt to establish an exact height for the waterfalls in this guide. Information was gathered from old Geological Survey of Canada maps, Natural Resources Canada topographical maps, and a form of extrapolation with the built-in altimeter on a Garmin GPS, as well as from the elevation profile on Google Earth, using its KML (Keyhole Markup Language). Being more specific would require expensive GPS equipment and knowledge in the use of such, not to mention that the beginning of a waterfall can be uncertain at best. To convert from metres to feet, multiply by approximately 3.3.

Best season: The best season to explore a waterfall is subjective. Choosing the best season to venture out to explore a waterfall is centred on personal preference. I enjoy autumn and therefore my preference is skewed. Fall, with its cooler temperatures and colours splashing the landscape, makes the exploration a welcoming adventure. During the summer months, many of the waterfalls in New Brunswick experience periods of low water. It is important to note that, while the watercourse may still have water, the waterfall itself may have diminished.

New Brunswickers are gifted with numerous accessible waterfalls, making all seasons attractive for waterfalling. Waterfalls such as Pabineau or Tetagouche are within minutes of Bathurst and provide a timely distraction from daily life. The optimum season in New Brunswick tends to be from May to November, based on the part of the province where the waterfall is located. The warmer Fundy ecosystem may provide enthusiasts with opportunities to visit falls as early as April and as late as December. In the northern section of the province, the season is shortened somewhat by earlier snowfalls and later spring thaws. Our waterfalls freeze over and are covered with snow by mid-winter, offering a different waterfall experience. For example, Belinda and I like to snowshoe out to Hays Falls to enjoy a light snack, have a cup of tea, and on the chance occasion, watch climbing enthusiasts scale the ice face; it is a wonderful mid-winter escape.

My advice is simple. Visit waterfalls during late spring or, if this is not possible, visit before the middle of summer to reduce the likelihood of a dried-up waterfall. Springtime runoff from the previous winter can last throughout most of the season and even into summer at times, depending on the early rains. Unless a record-breaking drought has occurred, which is unlikely in New Brunswick, every waterfall in this guide will be flowing. Beyond the middle of June, however, each waterfall's character begins to change. To prevent disappointment, making a quick check with the Department of Natural Resources district office in the area you intend to visit or contacting a local outfitter is a very practical planning tip.

The following are some general guidelines that have proven useful:
- Mountain brooks are likely to dry up faster than lowland rivers.
- The waterfalls of northern New Brunswick survive far longer in summer than do the falls of the southern section.
- Falls at the base of a mountain are likely to remain longer than falls located halfway up a trail leading to the summit.
- Snowy winters mean longer waterfall seasons during the warmer months.
- If you are hiking along a stream to a waterfall and not much water is flowing, you run the risk of visiting a dried-up waterfall.
- Expect a normally seasonal waterfall to be roaring with power for up to one week after a day of heavy rain. You are guaranteed a great show if you visit within three days of a storm.

Seasonality is not always a terrible thing. Differences in water flow can create new sparkling personalities and character changes in waterfalls. I suggest making every season your waterfall season.

Access: The waterfalls in the guide are accessed through various types of terrain, ranging from easy to downright strenuous. Similar to the original guide, the updated version offers a wide range of hiking challenges for enthusiasts. Following are the types of access to the waterfalls:

Trail: Hikes have official or well-used unofficial trails leading to the waterfall.

Roadside: Waterfalls are located within metres of designated roads.

Bushwhack: Accessing the waterfalls requires walking through thick woods and clearcuts. Depending on the type and age of the forest, it can be easy or difficult to push through the vegetation. In some cases, there are extreme ascents or descents in a gorge while holding onto trees and rocks.

River walk: If you are into waterfalling, this is a prerequisite. Associated with some waterfalls are rock outcrops and cliffs that will force you to walk in or close to the water, and there will be instances when getting your feet wet is required.

Shore walk: Included are a few waterfalls that require walking along a coastal shore. It is important to consult tide charts before heading out on these hikes, especially for the walks along the Bay of Fundy, where the water level changes up to 16 m between low and high tide.

Names for the **sources** of the waterfalls in the guide are verified with Natural Resources Canada topographical maps and the NRC Geographical Name search engine. In instances when there were no names for a lake, river, stream, or brook, I relied on information from locals or used nearby geographical features.

The one-way **distance** from trailhead to waterfall was determined using GPS Tracks and Google Earth measurement tools. The distance hiked will vary, depending on the navigational skills of the user and the route chosen. All distances are indicated in metric measurements: 1 km is roughly equivalent to 0.62 miles and 1 m is roughly equivalent to 1.1 yards.

Difficulty: Trails to the waterfalls in this book are categorized by the challenges encountered during the hike. Please note that what I suggest as moderate may be more difficult for others or vice versa. Hike difficulty is very dependent on the physical condition of the hike and of the person. There are four levels:

Easy: Waterfalls in this category are perfect for families with young children and individuals with mobility challenges.

Moderate: These are waterfalls that may not have a defined path, have moderate elevation changes throughout the length of the hike, and/or may require some bushwhacking. For the most part, a person of average fitness should have no issues.

Difficult: Any of the waterfalls rated difficult in this guide should be seriously considered before venturing out. There is little doubt that a good fitness level and familiarity with a forest setting are required, and navigational skills are essential. Therefore, evaluating all information is necessary before attempting one of these hikes.

Extreme: A few of the access hikes are considered extreme and should not be attempted lightly. Bushwhacking and navigating extreme elevation changes of up to 100 m in river gorges are required. As well, these waterfalls are in remote areas, so only fit and experienced hikers should attempt to reach them.

25. The Jaws (bonus fall)

The **elevation** category is a positive change from the first guide. Elevations will help the enthusiast with the decision to hike to a particular waterfall or not. In some cases, the trail is relatively flat but can change dramatically in elevation over a short section. A prime example is Upper Falls, Third Vault Brook in Fundy National Park: the last 500 m of this almost 4 km hike are extremely steep.

Hiking time is relative to physical fitness and familiarity with a forest setting, and can change based on whether hiking a trail, bushwhacking through dense forest, or crossing through a clearcut. It is important to have an understanding of variables like elevation changes. I am very quick and usually average a 10 minute per kilometre pace on a good trail, but my time can double or triple when bushwhacking and taking time to check my GPS and note my surroundings. Daylight hours are an important aspect to keep in mind, as nightfall in a forest arrives roughly 30 minutes earlier than in open areas. All hiking times in the guide are two-way, with additional time added for the encumbrances noted above. It is important to manage time while in the woods.

Land ownership: I attempted to identify land ownership for these waterfalls and trails, using various information assets such as Service New Brunswick's GeoNB and Land Grant Maps. The fact of the matter is that watercourses are not defined by man-made boundaries and, therefore, may flow from Crown (public) lands into private ones along their length. Some watercourses, but not many, have riparian rights that limit access, usually on larger rivers where salmon pools are hotly contested and protected. In this guide, only waterfalls not interfering with the property owner's enjoyment were used. GeoNB does not provide personal information on land owners, and no attempt by the publisher or myself was made to contact them. In some instances, the property is a large tract of woodland with the owners or company residing in another province or country.

Fees and permits: There are several waterfalls where nominal fees are required, such as those located in Mount Carleton Provincial Park, the Fundy Trail Parkway, and Fundy National Park. Irving Woodlands charges a fee to visit Fall Brook Falls in the Southwest Miramichi area, and Acadian Timber charges for access to their woodlands.

Maps: Included with each waterfall description is the associated Natural Resources Canada NTS (National Topographic System) map name. Also included are detailed maps of the waterfall access with enhanced directions. The reader should be able to follow the descriptive trail directions using each map.

Nearby waterfall(s): Associated with each waterfall are nearby waterfalls that are suggested as adjunct sites to visit while travelling to a particular area. You can also use my first waterfall guide to identify additional waterfalls to visit.

Cellphone coverage: Coverage was checked at each waterfall. It is safe to assume there is no coverage within a deep ravine where there is no direct line of sight to a communication tower. With this said, it was surprising to find areas that I thought would have service and were outside the coverage areas instead. A short drive to an elevated area was required to check connectivity. For this project, Telus Mobile Services were utilized.

Finding the trailhead: In most instances, the trailhead coordinates are as close as possible to the waterfall to minimize hiking, except where there is an excellent trail or gravel road to hike. There are roads used for logging that require vehicles with higher clearance. In these cases, a long hike may be required. In all cases, the distance from a major road was measured using GPS Tracks and/or Google Earth. It must be noted that trailheads may disappear or be altered due to forestry operations, but GPS coordinates will not change. Trust the coordinates.

Trailhead: Trailhead locations are indicated by GPS coordinates. In some situations, it is a general area such as a roadside location or the end of a logging road in a clearcut. An excellent contrast is between Falls Brook Falls in Restigouche, which has its trailhead at the end of a logging road within a clearcut, and Falls Brook Falls in Madawaska, which has a designated and marked trailhead.

Waterfall: The GPS coordinates for waterfall locations are in the most common format of degree, minutes, seconds. To provide a correct reading, the distance used was measured to the closest point accessible to the waterfall. Depending on the density of the forest canopy and the steepness of the ravine and its surroundings, the coordinates might be slightly less precise.

The hike: This narrative is in two sections. The first describes the hiking directions to the falls and any information or conditions concerning the hike. The second is a general description of the area, including a brief historical or geographical sketch and personal observations, such as the best location from which to photograph the waterfall. It would be uninteresting if the guide led only to known waterfalls with groomed trails. Many of the waterfalls require bushwhacking and crossing clearcuts. I will be honest: I prefer bushwhacking to clearcuts. Clearcuts are difficult to walk across, especially when the grass is high, because the footing is difficult, and they are open to direct sunlight. Bushwhacking is inevitable due to the nature of the prize, but with a tree canopy, it is cooler.

Bonus fall(s): The bonus information on waterfalls and other features does not include details such as maps with a trail or images, but it does include GPS coordinates. It was decided to leave the research on these trails to the enthusiasts who may want to venture further.

Mapping: All latitude and longitude coordinates in this guide are recorded using NAD83 (North American Datum of 1983) and are displayed as degree, minutes, seconds. There are various online sites to convert to other coordinate systems, such as UTM (Universal Transverse Mercator) or decimal degrees. All the maps featured in this guide have a north heading at the top.

Rating: This guide has a rating system between one and five. Any waterfall rating is bound to be somewhat subjective. My ratings are very much dependent on conditions such as time of year and water flow. A waterfall rated four in May could score as low as one in August, when the water level in many brooks and streams is depleted. Another governing factor is personal preference. I might rate a waterfall a five that someone else would consider only a three or four. However, you can count on any waterfall rated five in this book – especially if it is also identified as highly recommended – as being pretty special. My rating system is as follows:

1. **Uninspiring** – only interesting to diehard waterfall enthusiasts
2. **Modest** – nice scenery
3. **Good** – pretty enough to make a special trip
4. **Very Good** – outstanding scenery
5. **Exceptional** – an awe-inspiring, must-see waterfall

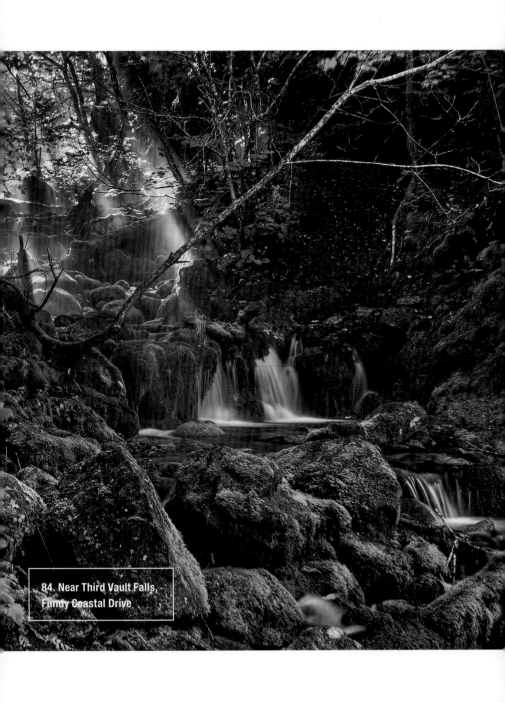

84. Near Third Vault Falls, Fundy Coastal Drive

Safety and Other Considerations

Waterfalling is not an activity that should be undertaken casually. It is mostly safe and enjoyable, but there is an element of risk. It gives me great concern when I see people hiking to a waterfall wearing flip-flops instead of good footwear. It is trouble waiting to happen! This guide cannot inform the user of every situation; it can only provide guidance. Every effort has been made to ensure that all the information in this book is correct, but it is up to the book's user to remain safe – always prepare and take precautions. Common sense should be the ultimate guide, but some of the main rules, like knowing when to turn around, are below.

Waterfalls are located in potential risky areas that should be treated as such. Exercise caution and prepare well, regardless of trail ratings, due to various conditions that can exist such as loose rocks, slippery surroundings, or excessive amounts of moisture. Many waterfalls in this guide are relatively close to a parking area or highway. There are others, such as East Branch Point Wolfe River Falls in Albert County, that are off the beaten track and require a bushwhack and strenuous climbs up and down steep escarpments to appreciate their beauty. Due to the inherent danger of injury or mishap, preparation is required. Also note that, even though GPS coordinates are provided, understanding how they relate to the real world is essential.

Establish a turnaround time. This is essential when hiking into an unfamiliar area, especially in late autumn. As mentioned earlier, evening settles in very quickly in the woods. Making it back to the trailhead can be achieved by abiding to a pre-established schedule. In November, several years ago, my son, three of my friends, and I decided to explore Walton Glen Gorge and the Eye of the Needle. We decided on a turnback time of 3:00 p.m. due to the early onset of darkness. It was a difficult decision to turn around at that time, as we had not yet located the Eye of the Needle. Regardless, we turned back and made it to the truck just before dark. It was my first time leading an excursion, and it provided the valuable lesson to plan and to follow the plan. Do not exceed your abilities or the abilities of the group – throttle back expectations to suit the weakest. Inform someone of your plan and follow that plan. Provide them with information such as vehicle type and license plate, as well as a map with your route. The difficulty ratings in this book are meant only as a general guide. The user is the best guide; if unsure about the route ahead, turn back.

The following list has items that are strongly recommended to carry with you:

- Guide book
- Compass, map, and GPS with extra batteries
- Drinking water and energy snacks or protein bars
- Small first aid kit in a fanny pack
- Sunblock and bug repellent
- Knife and rope
- Bucksaw (in case the access road is blocked by deadfalls)
- Whistle
- Marking tape if bushwhacking (to mark a path in case your GPS fails)
- Walking stick, plastic sheet, matches or fire starter (optional)

This may seem like common sense, but if you respect the property and the owner when crossing **private property**, even the absentee owners will respect you. Negative actions reflect unfavourably on all hikers.

Carry out what is carried in. Always carry a plastic shopping bag to pick up trash or litter. Eventually everyone will get the message, and the area will remain clean. It is amazing the garbage that can be found in the most remote locations.

Wear appropriate footwear. Invest in good hiking boots that are easily dried. No matter the weather or terrain, they will get wet and muddy. Good boots will allow for a comfortable hike, reduce the chance of injury, and not leave legs as tired.

It is important to understand the various **seasons**. In New Brunswick, we enjoy hunting seasons. Many people are unaware that bear hunting season is in the spring, and moose and deer seasons run from late September until early November. Meanwhile bird and small game seasons run at various times in the fall and winter. It is prudent to check with the Department of Natural Resources to determine the beginning and end of each hunting season and to wear hunter orange. A lightweight orange vest can be worn year-round while waterfalling and hiking. It is just

Lady slipper

a good habit to wear orange, as it makes it easier to see people in the forest. An added tool should be a whistle. The sound carries for a long distance and can help Search and Rescue personnel to find a lost person.

We live in New Brunswick, so if you don't like the weather at the moment, just wait a while, and it will change. It is always prudent to check the forecast before heading out. My preference is overcast weather with a chance of light rain, but only because of the photography since a cloudy day will enhance the quality and richness of colours in the images. As for camera settings, I have a personal recipe that I have adopted and improved over continual practice.

I suggest searching the internet for information on photographing waterfalls.

Encounters seldom happen with a **black bear** or **moose**. That is not to say they will never occur, but animals tend to go out of their way to stay away from humans, and we should do the same. In all my time in the forest, I have never encountered a bear face-

Agaricales

to-face — or a moose either, for that matter — but I have seen them from afar. My only close encounter was with a coyote who walked directly toward me while I was sitting on the tailgate of my truck, enjoying a cup of tea. Once it acknowledged my presence, it slipped quietly away into the brush. Remember, we are in their natural surroundings and should respect that they are wild animals. Carry bear spray and a walking stick. Use the stick to tap rocks and trees to alert animals of your presence. Beyond carrying a weapon, the only universally recommended items for defense are spray repellents containing capsaicin (hot pepper liquid), which are commercially available to discourage bold bears. These repellents are effective and will *not* injure the bear's eyes or make the bear aggressive. CAUTION! Care must be taken when using these products. Be sure to follow label instructions. There is ample information on the Department of Natural Resources website, as well as on the internet in general. Education and awareness are essential.

Since approximately eighty-five percent of New Brunswick is forest, there is a high probability of **blackflies, mosquitoes, deer flies, and ticks**. Planning for them on early spring hikes will eliminate some of the discomforts. Unfortunately, over the warmer summer months, you can expect to be attacked. Fly dope with DEET will help keep bugs away, but DEET is not always the best solution, so an alternative is to wear long sleeves and pants to protect your arms and legs.

Lyme disease, carried by the blacklegged tick, has become widespread in Southern New Brunswick and is beginning to move northward. The best prevention for this disease is to wear long pants and long-sleeved shirts, preferably in lightweight, breathable materials for comfort. Even though it is not fashionable, fasten tops securely at the neck and tuck the pant legs into your socks, making a seal from neck to toe. Once back home, check your clothing and body for any sign of ticks. A tick can transmit Lyme disease when attached for more than twenty-four to thirty-six hours. One indication can be a bull's-eye rash, and the following symptoms can occur: fever, headaches, fatigue, muscle aches, and joint pain. If these symptoms occur, contact a doctor. For more information, check the website for the Office of the Chief Medical Officer of Health at https://www2.gnb.ca/content/gnb/en/departments/ocmoh.html.

Poison ivy

Shiny, three-leaved **poison ivy** can be present along a trail or forest edge. The leaf consists of three pointed leaflets, with the middle leaflet having a much longer stalk than the two side ones. It is a climbing plant, belonging to the sumac family, and is extremely adaptable in both its habitat and growth. To prevent exposure, wear long pants and long-sleeved shirts to ensure that no area of the skin is exposed to the sap of the adult plant. To protect against contact, you can also wear light-weight garden gloves. Just remember the old proverb: leaves of three, let it be!

Invasive **giant hogweed** has established a foothold in limited areas of New Brunswick. Giant hogweed can reach a height of 1.5 m to 5 m. According to New Brunswick's Office of the Chief Medical Officer of Health (Public Health) website: "Hogweed has a hollow stem with purplish blotches and is considered a public health hazard. It can be harmful to people if in contact with it. The watery sap has toxins that, after exposure to sunlight, can cause skin inflammation, burns and a rash. Note that if the sap comes in contact with the eye, it can cause temporary blindness."

Although **GPS coordinates and maps** are provided in the guide, it is important to understand how to read and relate the information to real-world locations. A good practice is to search the GPS coordinates in Google Earth, trace out your hike, and save the map on an iPhone and/or print it for reference. Make a mental note of your surroundings while hiking to a waterfall. Carry marking tape to mark a path, just in case the batteries on the GPS fail or satellite connection is lost. It will provide a sense of security and may be needed later. Forest trails can change during forestry operations, and what was familiar one year may not be the same the following season. Note that there are many routes in this guide that are prolonged bushwhacks and require the user to understand how to use a GPS and read maps. For further education, check out information on the internet or in your local library.

Trust your instincts! Due to their surroundings, waterfalls are located in risky places. Please be very careful when visiting all waterfalls. Although this guide provides accurate and easy-to-follow directions, as well as GPS coordinates, there could be natural or human changes to locations and conditions.

Waterfalls at a Glance

The following table provides an overview of all the waterfalls in this guide and their key features, as well as information about difficulty and cellphone coverage.

Rating: **1** = Uninspiring   **2** = Modest   **3** = Good   **4** = Very Good   **5** = Exceptional

Type: **C** = Cascade   **D** = Drop   **F** = Fan   **S** = Slide   **T** = Tiered

Height: The height of the fall in metres

Season: **SP** = Spring   **S** = Summer   **F** = Fall   **W** = Winter   **YR** = Year-round

Access: **T** = Trail   **R** = Roadside   **B** = Bushwhack   **RW** = River walk   **SW** = Shore walk

Distance: Distance is provided as **one way**, in kilometres or metres

Difficulty: **E** = Easy   **M** = Moderate   **D** = Difficult   **X** = Extreme

Cell: The availability of cellphone coverage: **Yes** = Y   **No** = N

Waterfall	Rating	Type	Height	Season	Access	Distance (one way)	Diff.	Cell
ACADIAN COASTAL DRIVE								
1. Fisher Hill Falls	2	D, S	4	SP, F	T	1.3 km	E	N
2. Indian Falls	2	C	1.5	SP, S, F	T	267 m	E-M	N
3. Buck Falls	3	C	3	SP, S, F	T	1.1 km	E-M	N
4. Rainbow Falls	3	D	6	SP, S, F	T	471 m	M	N
5. Roger Brook Falls	4	T	5	S, F	B, RW	736 m	M-D	N
6. Pabineau Falls	4	C	8	SP, S, F	T	10 m	E	Y
7. Armstrong Brook Falls	1	T	7	SP, F	T, B	1.9 km	M-D	N
8. Tetagouche Falls	4	D	10	S, F	T	352 m	E-M	Y
9. Nigadoo River Falls	3	C	8	SP, S, F	T	646 m	E	Y
10. Chute de la Rivière aux Ormes	1	C	3	SP, F	B	346 m	M	Y
11. Antinouri Lake Brook Falls	2	S	9	S, F	T, B	1.9 km	M-D	N
12. Nash Creek Falls	2	T	3	SP, F	B	400 m	M-D	Y
13. Secret Falls	3	T	2	S, F	RW	871 m	M	N

Waterfall	Rating	Type	Height	Season	Access	Distance (one way)	Diff.	Cell
APPALACHIAN RANGE ROUTE								
14. Cigar Falls	3	D	5	SP, F	T, B	569 m	E-M	Y
15. Shipyard Brook Falls	1	C	3	SP	SW	203 m	E	Y
16. Christopher Brook Falls	1	C	1.5	S, F	T	29 m	E	Y
17. Mill Brook Slide	1	S	5	SP, F	T	30 m	E	Y
18. Grog Brook Falls	2	C	3	SP, F	T	3 km	E	N
19. Falls Brook Falls (Restigouche)	5	T	10	S, F	T, B	420 m	M	N
20. Whites Brook Falls	5	D, T	20	S, F	T	4.4 km	M-D	N
21. Clearwater Brook Falls	2	C	10	SP, F	B	163 m	M	N
22. Eighteen Mile Brook Falls	3	T	8	S, F	RW, B	767 m	D	N
23. Southeast Gorge Falls	3	D	3	S, F	B	579 m	M-D	N
24. Williams Brook Falls	3	T	3	SP, S, F	T	243 m	E	N
25. Odell River Falls	4	D	13	S, F	B, T	1.4 km	M-D	N
26. Maggie's Falls	5	D, T	Various	SP, S, F	T	1.14 km	E	N
RIVER VALLEY SCENIC DRIVE								
27. Falls Brook Falls (Madawaska)	4	D	10	S, F	T	460 m	E	N
28. Gagne Falls	4	D	7	S, F	T	173 m	E	N
29. Chute de la Quisibis	4	D	14	S, F	T	807 m	E-M	N
30. Four Falls	4	T	Various	S, F	T	205 m	E	Y
31. Craig Falls	4	D	6	S, F	T	434 m	E	N
32. Briggs Millpond Falls	3	C	2	SP, F	R	25 m	E	Y
33. Jennings Falls	4	T	8	SP, S, F	T	107 m	E-M	Y
34. Millseat Falls	2	T	5	SP, S, F	R	9.1 m	E	Y
35. Gibson Creek Falls	3	T	10	SP, S, F	T	220 m	E	Y
36. Hays Falls	5	F	24	YR	T	1.5 km	E-M	Y
37. Eel River Falls	3	D	2.5	S, F	T	2.4 km	E	Y
38. Sullivan Creek Falls	5	C	20	SP, F	B	1.2 km	M	N
39. Big Falls (Shogomoc)	5	C	5	SP, S, F	T, B	1.1 km	M	Y

Waterfall	Rating	Type	Height	Season	Access	Distance (one way)	Diff.	Cell
40. Coac Stream Falls	5	T	21	SP, F	T	2.2 km	E-M	Y
41. Mactaquac Stream Falls	3	C	8	S, F	T	2 km	E	Y
42. Howland Falls	3	T	11	YR	T	111 m	E	Y
43. Lower Joslin Creek Falls	4	D	6	YR	T	71 m	E-M	Y
44. Split Rock Falls	4	C	6	SP, S, F	T	1.1 km	M	Y
45. Pete Brook Falls	2	D	5	SP, F	T, RW	822 m	E-M	Y
46. Carrow Brook Falls	2	F	5	SP, F	T	287 m	E-M	Y
47. Scribner Brook Falls	2	D	1.5	SP, F	T	42 m	E	Y
48. Raggedy Ass Falls	4	T	Various	SP, F	T	658 m	E	Y
49. Hubble Brook Falls	2	T	5	SP, F	T	56 m	E	Y
50. Sand Brook Falls	3	D	3	SP, F	T	199 m	E	Y
51. Mooneys Ridge Falls	3	C	6	SP, F	T, B	413 m	E-M	Y
52. Welsford Falls	5	F	10	SP, S, F	T	342 m	E-M	Y
53. Cunningham Creek Falls	3	C	8	S, F	T, B	467 m	M-D	Y
54. Wyman Mills Falls	2	S	3	SP, S, F	T	148 m	E	N
FUNDY COASTAL DRIVE								
55. Saint Paddy's Falls	4	F	6	SP, F	T	425 m	E	Y
56. Hidden Falls	2	C	5	SP, F	T, B	287 m	E-M	Y
57. Red Rock Stream Falls	2	S	3	SP, F	T	101 m	E	Y
58. Knights Mill Brook Falls	3	T	4	SP, F	R, T	1.3 km	E	Y
59. New River Falls	3	C	4	SP, F	T	174 m	E	Y
60. Keyhole Falls	5	T	6	S, F	T	1.2 km	E-M	Y
61. Little Lepreau River Falls	2	C	3	SP, S, F	T	99 m	E	Y
62. Moose Creek Falls	3	C	3	SP, F	T, B	727 m	E-M	Y
63. First Falls, West Branch Musquash River	2	C	5	YR	T	41 m	E	Y
64. Perch Brook Falls	2	T	3	SP, F	T	48 m	E	Y

Waterfall	Rating	Type	Height	Season	Access	Distance (one way)	Diff.	Cell
65. Kierstead Mountain Falls	3	C	8	SP, F	T	403 m	E-M	Y
66. Back Settlement Road Falls	4	F	4	SP, F	T	314 m	E	N
67. First Falls, Porter Brook (Saint John)	4	D	10	SP, F	T, B	2.6 km	M-D	N
68. Big Rody Brook Falls	5	D	5	SP, S, F	B	567 m	D-X	N
69. Little Rody Brook Falls	5	D	4	SP, S, F	B	431 m	D-X	N
70. Pine Brook Falls	3	D	5	SP, F	B	863 m	M-D	N
71. Hells Kitchen Falls	5	T	10	SP, S, F	B	1.32 km	M-D	N
72. Hemlock Brook Falls	4	D	12	SP, F	T, B	1.3 km	M-D	N
73. Bonnell Brook Falls	3	T	9	SP, S, F	T, B	3 km	M-D	N
74. Parlee Brook Falls	3	D	4	SP, F	B, RW	721 m	M	N
75. Long Beach Brook Falls	2	S	4	SP, F	T	779 m	E-M	Y
76. Walton Glen Brook Falls	4	T	35	SP, S, F	T	1.14 km	M-D	N
77. Wallace Falls	3	D	6	SP, S, F	T	266 m	E-M	N
78. Tweedledum and Tweedledee Falls	3	T	12	SP, F	T, SW, B	4.9 km	M-D	N
79. Goose Creek Falls	4	D	12	S, F	B, RW	1.6 km	M-D	N
80. Sproul Settlement Falls	4	T	14	SP, F	B, T	1 km	M-D	N
81. Pollett River Falls	2	C	5	YR	T	64 m	M	Y
82. East Branch Point Wolfe River Falls	4	C	4	S, F	T, B	1.4 km	M-X	N
83. Haley Brook Falls	3	T	4	SP, F	B	341 m	M	N
84. Upper Falls, Third Vault Brook	4	D	20	SP, S, F	T, B, RW	3.8 km	M-X	N
85. Beaver Brook Falls	4	F	25	SP, F	T, B	803 m	M-D	Cell
86. Bough Brook Falls	3	T	3	SP, F	B	469 m	M	Y
87. Midway Falls	2	C	4	SP, F	B, RW	753 m	M	Y
88. Slacks Cove Falls	2	C	3	SP, F	T	48 m	E	Y

Waterfall	Rating	Type	Height	Season	Access	Distance (one way)	Diff.	Cell
MIRAMICHI RIVER ROUTE								
89. Sandburn Brook Falls	2	T	3	SP, F	B	362 m	M	N
90. Little Sheephouse Brook Falls	4	D	10	SP, S, F	T	234 m	E	Y
91. Mullin Stream Falls	3	D	4	SP, F	T	1.2 km	M	Y
92. Indiantown Brook Falls	3	D	2	SP, F	T, B	601 m	D	Y
93. Devils Brook Falls	2	T	3	SP, F	T	92 m	E	N
94. Libbies Falls	5	T	8	SP, F	T	3.3 km	E-M	N
95. Bartholomew River Falls	3	D	3	SP, F	T	2.2 km	E-M	N
96. Fall Brook Falls (York)	5	D	33	S, F	T	742 m	E-M	N
97. Porter Brook Falls (Northumberland)	2	C	2	SP, F	T	55 m	E	Y
98. Chase Brook Falls	2	D	4	SP, F	T	74 m	E	Y
99. Midland Falls	1	C	3	SP, S, F	T	266 m	E	Y
100. Penniac Cascade	1	C	Various	SP, F	R, B	61 m	M	Y

31. Craig Falls

ACADIAN COASTAL DRIVE

Dalhousie 12

QUEBEC

13 10

11 9

Chaleur Bay

Shippagan

7 8 *Bathurst*

2,3 6 *Tracadie-Sheila*

4,5

Gulf of
St. Lawrence

1. Fisher Hill Falls
2. Indian Falls
3. Buck Falls
4. Rainbow Falls
5. Roger Brook Falls
6. Pabineau Falls
7. Armstrong Brook Falls
8. Tetagouche Falls
9. Nigadoo River Falls
10. Chute de la Rivière aux Ormes
11. Antinouri Lake Brook Falls
12. Nash Creek Falls
13. Secret Falls

Miramichi

Richibucto

PRINCE
EDWARD
ISLAND

1

Northumberland Strait

Shediac

Oromocto

Moncton

Sackville

Sussex

NOVA SCOTIA

Bay of Fundy

Saint John

Acadian Coastal Drive

The Acadian Coastal Drive edges the entire east coast of New Brunswick from Aulac, near the border with Nova Scotia, to the village of Charlo on Chaleur Bay. From the Buctouche sand dunes to the rolling hills of the Chaleur Uplands, this route boasts many natural wonders. The geography of New Brunswick is extremely varied, and this is evident along the Acadian Coastal Drive. Geologically, the region is comprised of two zones. The largest is the New Brunswick Lowlands (part of the Maritimes Basin), a chevron-shaped landmass of sandstone and conglomerate rock formed by the sediments of an ancient river. The lowlands stretch from the Nova Scotia border to Bathurst. This includes the Acadian Peninsula and protrudes inland beyond Fredericton, including portions of Northumberland and York Counties. The entire region is tilted toward the coastline. South of the Southwest Miramichi River, rivers and streams are brownish in colour due to the many marshes and wetlands. Ecologically, the area is dominated by peat bogs. This fact, coupled with geological composition, means that there are few waterfalls of significant size. This all changes north of the Southwest Miramichi River, where the numerous tributaries are mountain-fed, ensuring the rivers are clear and cold.

From Bathurst to Charlo, a second geological zone dominates the landscape. The Chaleur Uplands, identified by New Brunswick Natural Resources and Energy Development as part of the Tobique-Chaleur Zone, were formed by continental convergence that folded the land back on itself in successive ridges and is part of the Appalachian Mountains. The region runs west to east in a succession of mountain ridges and deep valleys. Here, the Appalachian mountain range descends, submerging into Chaleur Bay in a series of folds. In a stark contrast with the rivers to the south, the fast-moving rivers of this portion of the route have incised deep valleys or gulches into the tableland, producing such spectacular waterfalls as Nigadoo River Falls and Tetagouche Falls. This area also includes rivers such as the Benjamin and Jacquet that feature an almost continuous series of rapids and waterfalls. This section of the route contains numerous post-glacial waterfalls. Such waterfalls were formed when debris from the last ice age blocked the original river. The water was then forced to flow around the encumbrance, forming a waterfall as the river dropped back into the original channel.

6. Pabineau Falls

1. Fisher Hill Falls

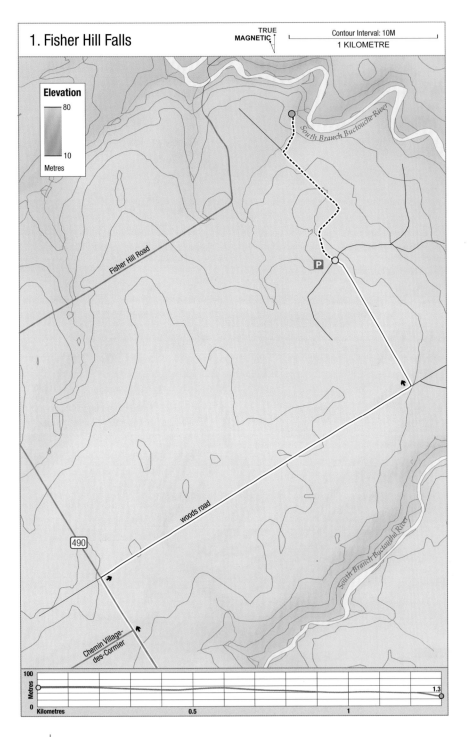

1. Fisher Hill Falls

Type: Drop, slide
Height: 4 m
Best season(s): Spring, fall
Access: Trail
Source: Unknown
Distance (one way): 1.3 km
Difficulty: Easy

Rating: 2
Hiking time: 30 minutes
Land ownership: Crown
Map: NTS 021I07 Bouctouche
Nearby waterfall(s): N/A
Cellphone coverage: N

Finding the trailhead: From Route 126 (road to Rogersville), take Indian Mountain Road and drive 10 km to the intersection with Route 490. Turn left and head north toward Bass River. Drive approximately 15 km through small settlements until Gladeside and coordinates 46°19'38.3" N, 64°54'27.3" W. Turn east (right) onto the woods road and continue along this road to the trailhead, where there is ample space to park. The road is dusty when dry, but becomes slick and muddy after a rain. There are ruts and puddles along the drive, and beyond the trailhead, the road is grown-in with alders.

Trailhead: 46°20'45.3" N, 64°53'11.8" W **Waterfall:** 46°21'17.2" N, 64°53'24.2" W

The hike: From the trailhead, the walk is pleasant as the road descends to the brook. Just before the brook, turn right and follow the ATV trail, which eventually changes to a footpath that leads to the top of the falls. The waterfall is near the brook's confluence with the South Branch Buctouche River. This is a concealed treasure in the vast Maritimes Basin, a region consisting predominantly of sedimentary rock deposited by an ancient river, and is one of only a few notable waterfalls in Kent County. Since there is no definitive source, Fisher Hill Falls dries

to a dribble during the summer months, much as it had the morning that I arrived to photograph it. Nonetheless, the area around the waterfall was still draped in emerald green moss and emanated a fresh, woodsy aroma. It is certainly a waterfall to visit in the spring and autumn seasons or just after a few days of rain.

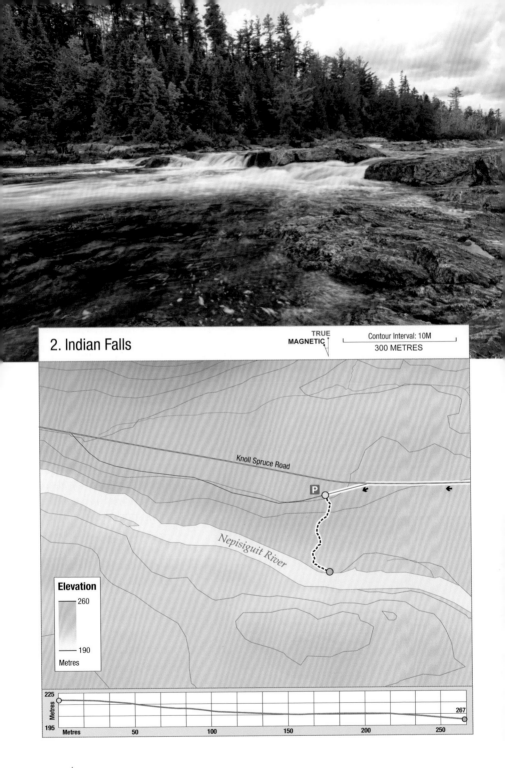

2. Indian Falls

TRUE
MAGNETIC

Contour Interval: 10M
300 METRES

Knoll Spruce Road

P

Nepisiguit River

Elevation

260

190

Metres

225
Metres
195

267

Metres 50 100 150 200 250

2. Indian Falls

Type: Cascade
Height: 1.5 m
Best season(s): Spring, summer, fall
Access: Trail
Source: Nepisiguit River
Distance (one way): 267 m
Difficulty: Easy to moderate

Rating: 2
Hiking time: 30 minutes
Land ownership: Crown
Map: NTS 021O08 California Lake
Nearby waterfall(s): Buck Falls, Roger Brook Falls, Rainbow Falls
Cellphone coverage: N

Finding the trailhead: From Miramichi, drive north on Route 8 toward Bathurst and take exit 304 to Route 430. Drive west on Route 430 away from Bathurst and toward Bathurst Mines for approximately 23 km. Just before reaching the community, turn right onto Knoll Spruce Road (known locally as the Nepisiguit River Road) at 47°26'01.0" N, 65°49'10.4" W. Continue on this gravel logging road roughly 38 km to the sign on the left side of the road, indicating Indian Falls. Pull off Knoll Spruce Road onto the old road on the left and park.

Trailhead: 47°22'01.0" N, 66°15'47.2" W   **Waterfall:** 47°21'54.1" N, 66°15'46.7" W

The hike: The trail is rather steep at the start but, once in the valley, meanders gently to the falls on the Nepisiguit River. Near the river there is a junction. The left-hand trail leads to the lower falls and the other leads to the upper falls and the beginning of an ancient and worn portage used to bypass the torrent. The Nepisguit is a major whitewater river in the province. Its name is derived from the Mi'gmaq word Ooinpegij'ooig, meaning "evil flowing water." Indian Falls adds excitement to this already beautiful New Brunswick river. At this location, the river gets progressively more boisterous as it runs through the rocky section that starts at the upper falls and culminates in a 1.5 m drop at Indian Falls.

Bonus feature: For a wilderness adventure, hike to the falls on the nearby Nepisiguit Mi'gmaq Trail. This section of the 147 km trail is accessed from Route 430. From the trailhead at 47°22'26.6" N, 66°04'16.4" W, it is a roughly 17 km one-way hike on one of New Brunswick's finest wilderness trails.

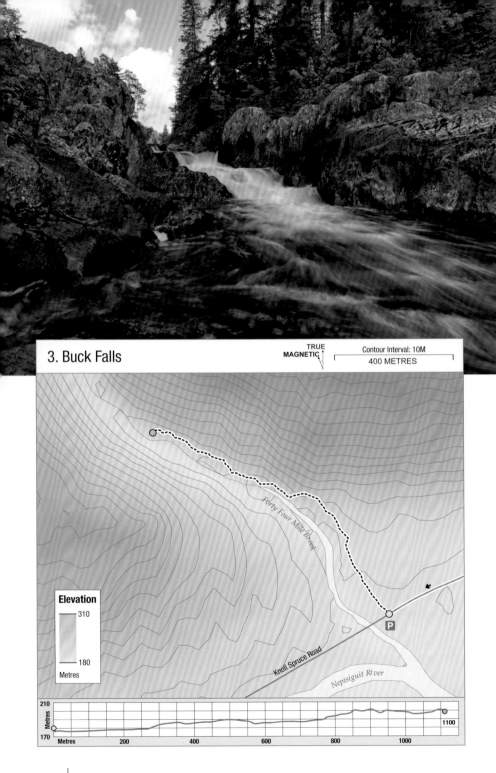

3. Buck Falls

TRUE
MAGNETIC

Contour Interval: 10M

400 METRES

Forty Four Mile Brook

Elevation

310

180

Metres

P

Knoll Spruce Road

Nepisiguit River

210

Metres

170

Metres   200   400   600   800   1000

1100

3. Buck Falls

Type: Cascade
Height: 3 m
Best season(s): Spring, summer, fall
Access: Trail
Source: Forty Four Mile Brook
Distance (one way): 1.1 km
Difficulty: Easy to moderate

Rating: 3
Hiking time: 40 minutes
Land ownership: Crown
Map: NTS 021O08 California Lake
Nearby waterfall(s): Rainbow Falls, Roger Brook Falls
Cellphone coverage: N

Finding the trailhead: From Miramichi, drive north on Route 8 toward Bathurst and take exit 304 to Route 430. Drive west on Route 430, away from Bathurst and toward Bathurst Mines, for approximately 23 km. Turn right onto Knoll Spruce Road (known locally as the Nepisiguit River Road) at 47°26'01.0" N, 65°49'10.4" W. Continue on this gravel logging road roughly 31 km to the trailhead. Opposite the trailhead is a picnic and parking area near the Nepisiguit River. The trailhead is located on the upper side of the main logging road and on the east side of the brook.

Trailhead: 47°23'34.9" N, 66°11'02.2" W   **Waterfall:** 47°23'54.6" N, 66°11'39.3" W

The hike: Buck Falls is situated 1.1 km up Forty Four Mile Brook. The trail is cleared of large downfalls and is well trodden as it leads up the eastern side of the brook through a mixed forest. There are areas that are overgrown with grass and ferns where the trail swings in near the brook, especially in summer. Along the trail and at the waterfall, there are large rock outcrops offering excellent vantage points. Note that the rocks become extremely slippery and dangerous when wet. The brook begins on the southern side of Camel Back Mountain and Mount Jack, and empties into the Nepisiguit River. The brook is named Forty Four Mile Brook because the confluence of the brook is located forty-four miles (seventy kilometres) upriver from Bathurst. Many brooks in New Brunswick were given mileage names as an identification point for lumbermen.

At the falls, the brook squeezes through a rocky outcrop, dropping into a large clear pool. There are several large boulders and a bench fashioned out of logs on which a person can sit, relax, reflect on life, and enjoy nature at its finest. The brook above the waterfall presents a wonderful panorama of the New Brunswick wilderness. The finest vantage point for photographs is on the opposite side of the waterfall.

4. Rainbow Falls

TRUE
MAGNETIC ↑

Contour Interval: 10M
400 METRES

South Branch

Forty Mile Brook

P

Whitebirch Road

Knoll Spruce Lake

Knoll Spruce Road

Elevation

— 350

— 160

Metres

300
Metres
200

471

Metres   100   200   300   400

4. Rainbow Falls

Type: Drop
Height: 6 m
Best season(s): Spring, summer, fall
Access: Trail
Source: South Branch Forty Mile Brook
Distance (one way): 471 m
Difficulty: Moderate

Rating: 3
Hiking time: 15 minutes
Land ownership: Crown
Map: NTS 021O08 California Lake
Nearby waterfall(s): Buck Falls, Roger Brook Falls
Cellphone coverage: N

Finding the trailhead: From Miramichi, drive north on Route 8 toward Bathurst and take exit 304 to Route 430. Drive west on Route 430, away from Bathurst and toward Bathurst Mines, for approximately 23 km. Turn right onto Knoll Spruce Road (known locally as the Nepisiguit River Road) at 47°26'01.0" N, 65°49'10.4" W. Continue on this gravel logging road about 28.5 km to the turnoff for the California Lake Crown Reserve at coordinates 47°24'08.3" N, 66°09'15.6" W. Turn right (north) and head up the hill to the trailhead, located on the righthand side of the road. There is plenty of space to park off to one side.

Trailhead: 47°24'57.7" N, 66°09'15.5" W **Waterfall:** 47°25'03.2" N, 66°08'57.3" W

The hike: The trailhead is marked and meanders down into the gorge for a distance of 490 m, emerging directly at the top of Rainbow Falls. Continue to the end of the trail; do not be fooled by the sound of the water cascading from a side stream on the hike down. The headwaters of South Branch Forty Mile Brook are situated in the lofty mountains that divide the Nepisiguit River system from the Jacquet and Tetagouche Rivers. Energized by several tributaries and small lakes located in these hills, the brook rushes enthusiastically toward the Nepisiguit River. Caught up in this enthusiasm is the beautiful Rainbow Falls, which drops into a large pool. The waterfall is nestled in a mixed forest and is orientated such that the late afternoon sun fails to reach the pool.

Bonus fall(s): There is an added attraction of a smaller set of falls located 20 m upriver from the main attraction.

5. Roger Brook Falls

Type: Tiered
Height: 5 m
Best season(s): Summer, fall
Access: Bushwhack, river walk
Source: Roger Brook
Distance (one way): 736 m
Difficulty: Moderate to difficult

Rating: 4
Hiking time: 30 minutes
Land ownership: Crown
Map: NTS 021O08 California Lake
Nearby waterfall(s): Sandburn Brook
Falls, Rainbow Falls
Cellphone coverage: N

Finding the trailhead: From Miramichi, drive north on Route 430 to the rural hamlet of Wayerton on the Northwest Miramichi River. Continue past Wayerton toward the defunct mine, where the road changes to gravel for the remainder of the drive. Located at the crest of the hill, just before the bridge spanning the Nepisiguit River, there is a logging road on the left (west) at 47°22'16.8" N, 66°04'09.4" W. Follow this road, known locally as the Old Otter Brook Road, as it swings north and down into the Nepisiguit River valley. At the bottom of the hill, the road crosses Roger Brook. Continue past the bridge to the trailhead,

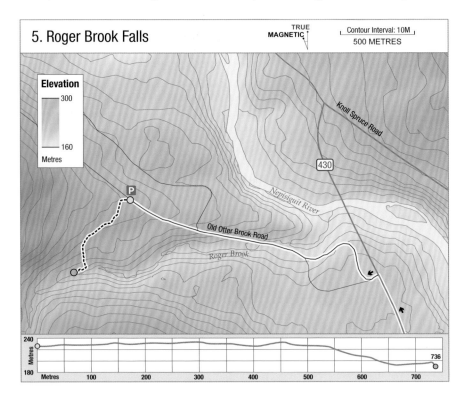

5. Roger Brook Falls

TRUE MAGNETIC

Contour Interval: 10M
500 METRES

located up the hill on the left. The total driving distance from Route 430 is 1.9 km. The trailhead begins at the edge of the clearcut.

Trailhead: 47°22'32.9" N, 66°05'28.2" W   **Waterfall:** 47°22'17.2" N, 66°05'45.6" W

The hike: There is no defined path, so bushwhacking and watercourse hiking are required. After crossing the clearcut, the hike follows an old woods road for a short time before a bushwhack is required to reach the brook. The ravine is pretty narrow, with jagged rock outcrops, so caution is required around the falls. With its genesis at Roger Lake, near the divide in the land between the Nepisiguit and Miramichi Rivers, Roger Brook trundles downward to join the Nepisiguit. Heavy harvesting practices are prevalent in and around this brook and further up the valley. Expect to find tree debris in the brook and waterfall as a result.

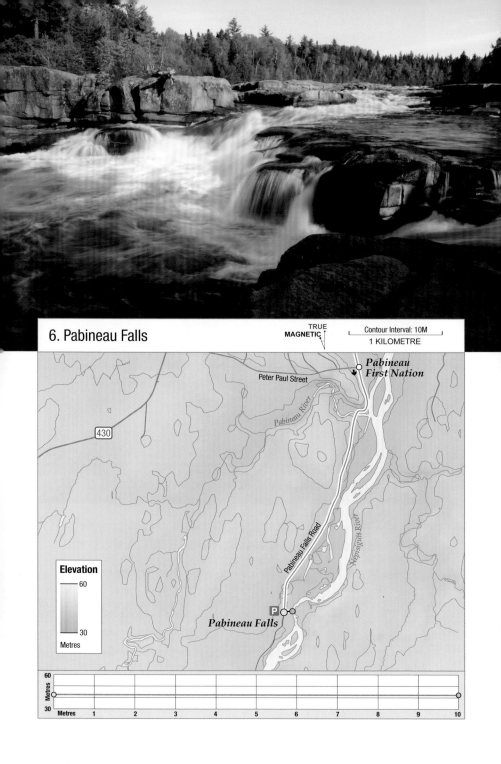

6. Pabineau Falls

TRUE
MAGNETIC

Contour Interval: 10M
1 KILOMETRE

Peter Paul Street

Pabineau First Nation

Pabineau River

430

Pabineau Falls Road

Nepisiguit River

Elevation
— 60

— 30
Metres

P
Pabineau Falls

60
Metres
30

Metres   1   2   3   4   5   6   7   8   9   10

6. Pabineau Falls

Type: Cascade
Height: 8 m
Best season(s): Spring, summer, fall
Access: Trail
Source: Nepisiguit River
Distance (one way): 10 m
Difficulty: Easy

Rating: 4
Hiking time: 1 minute
Land ownership: Crown
Map: NTS 021P12 Bathurst
Nearby waterfall(s): Tetagouche Falls, Armstrong Brook Falls
Cellphone coverage: Y

Finding the trailhead: From Miramichi, drive north on Route 8 toward Bathurst and take exit 304 to Route 430. Drive west on Route 430 away from Bathurst approximately 5 km toward Bathurst Mines until reaching a Y in the road. Take the road on the left to Pabineau First Nation and drive 5.5 km to the turnoff and the parking area immediately on your left. The trailhead and waterfall are at the same coordinates.

Trailhead: 47°30'29.0" N, 65°40'37.8" W
Waterfall: 47°30'29.0" N, 65°40'37.8" W

The hike: The crown jewel of waterfalls in the northeastern corner of our province is, without a doubt, the picturesque Pabineau Falls. The strong current, a series of very large rapids, and the grand open vistas adorned with mature pine trees create a popular site to visit, relax, and photograph.

The complicated Nepisiguit River is one of New Brunswick's major watercourses. At Pabineau Falls, the river squeezes through a labyrinth of granite boulders on its journey toward Chaleur Bay. For an outstanding view, take the trail along the river to a rock lookout. The area draws visitors into a false sense of security because of the flat rocks and the waterfall's breadth. During the spring freshet, though, this waterfall is dangerous – not because of its height, but due to the sheer volume, velocity, and ferocity of the river rushing through the channel. Caution is suggested. The entire area embracing the waterfall is at its best at the height of autumn colours in late September.

7. Armstrong Brook Falls

TRUE
MAGNETIC

Contour Interval: 10M
1 KILOMETRE

Armstrong Brook

old woods road

P

180

Elevation

280

180

Metres

300
Metres
220
Kilometres   0.5   1   1.5   1.9

7. Armstrong Brook Falls

Type: Tiered
Height: 7 m
Best season(s): Spring, fall
Access: Trail, bushwhack
Source: Armstrong Brook
Distance (one way): 1.9 km
Difficulty: Moderate to difficult

Rating: 1
Hiking time: 1 hour
Land ownership: Crown
Map: NTS 021P12 Bathurst
Nearby waterfall(s): Tetagouche Falls
Cellphone coverage: N

Finding the trailhead: From Route 11, take exit 310 in Bathurst (near the Atlantic Host Hotel and Tim Hortons) and drive away from the city on Route 180 toward South Tetagouche. After 24 km, turn right onto an old woods road at 47°34'55.3" N, 65°59'34.1" W. Drive roughly 610 m and park.

Trailhead: 47°35'11.7" N, 65°59'35.8" W   **Waterfall:** 47°35'59.8" N, 66°00'0.7" W

The hike: Since there is no path leading to the waterfall, familiarity with both the use of a GPS and hiking in the woods is essential. From the parking area, walk 670 m on the old woods road and turn right. Bushwhack the track due north through dense forest for roughly 1.2 km to the falls. Near the waterfall, there is a path leading down the righthand side of the ravine. The forest in this area is predominantly shade-intolerant hardwood of birch, poplar, and maple, indicative of past logging practices. The ravine is draped in a cover of softwoods, primarily cedar and spruce.

Armstrong Brook gathers water from a number of small bogans and streams, with sources located further up in the plateau as it slashes through the Chaleur Uplands until emptying into the Tetagouche River, just above Little Narrows. The brook has cut a significant ravine into the rock, and the waterfall is located in a fissure where three ridges intersect. The regularity of the plateau is broken only by a few hills and ridges rising slightly above the general elevation. To the east, increasing elevation makes the region more rugged, especially near Bathurst. The region is littered with significant bedrock outcroppings that, in combination with the numerous watersheds here, provide excellent waterfalls.

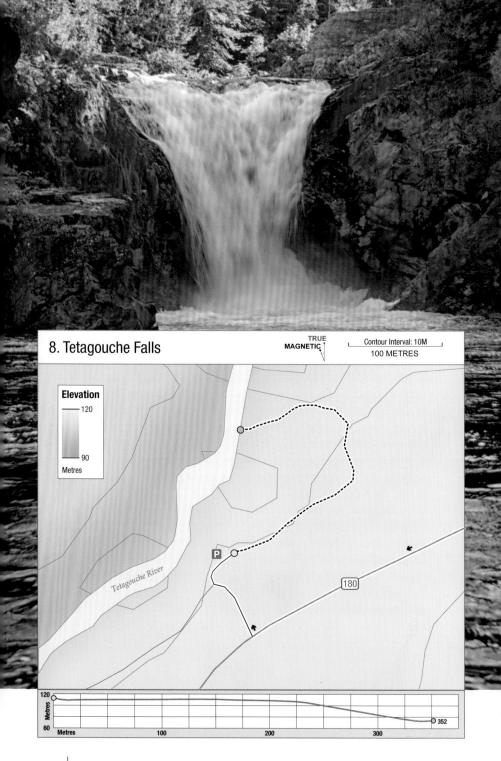

8. Tetagouche Falls

TRUE
MAGNETIC

Contour Interval: 10M
100 METRES

Elevation
120

90
Metres

Tetagouche River

P

180

120
Metres
60 352

Metres 100 200 300

8. Tetagouche Falls

Type: Drop
Height: 10 m
Best season(s): Summer, fall
Access: Trail
Source: Tetagouche River
Distance (one way): 352 m
Difficulty: Easy to moderate

Rating: 4
Hiking time: 20 minutes
Land ownership: Crown
Map: NTS 021P12 Bathurst
Nearby waterfall(s): Nigadoo River Falls, Pabineau Falls
Cellphone coverage: Y

Finding the trailhead: From Route 11, take exit 310 near the Atlantic Host Hotel and Tim Hortons in Bathurst and drive on Route 180 toward South Tetagouche and the falls. Drive roughly 9.5 km, looking for the entrance road and the parking area on the right at 47°36'59.1" N, 65°49'26.5" W.

Trailhead: 47°37'02.1" N, 65°49'27.0" W
Waterfall: 47°37'06.4" N, 65°49'27.1" W

The hike: For the best view of the falls and the old hydro dam, follow the trail down on the right side of the parking area. The trail is rather steep, so be prepared for an exhausting hike back up. It is an accessible area where the beauty and power of the falls excite tourists while continuing to attract local people from the greater Bathurst region.

With its headwaters at the Tetagouche Lakes, the Tetagouche is the second largest river in this region, after the Nepisiguit. During the spring freshet, mist rises from the tortured water as it plunges through the gorge. The force can be felt even 30 m downriver. There are remnants of a derelict hydro dam at the top of the falls, and of the old hydroelectric power generator that was built into the rocks, tucked away from the falls down in the gorge. The dam, constructed by local businessman John Leger in 1911, supplied power to Bathurst before the Nepisiguit dam was built by the Bathurst Company Ltd. (later Consolidated-Bathurst) for its paper mill in 1926. This powerful waterfall is not high, but the gorge is surrounded by vertical parapets, providing an impressive natural backdrop.

9. Nigadoo River Falls

Type: Cascade
Height: 8 m
Best season(s): Spring, summer, fall
Access: Trail
Source: Nigadoo River
Distance (one way): 646 m
Difficulty: Easy

Rating: 3
Hiking time: 20 minutes
Land ownership: Private
Map: NTS 021P12 Bathurst
Nearby waterfall(s): Pabineau Falls, Tetagouche Falls
Cellphone coverage: Y

Finding the trailhead: From Route 11 northwest of Bathurst, take exit 321. At the stop sign, turn left and drive away from the village of Nigadoo on Route 322 toward the community of Nicholas Denys. After approximately 1.5 km, turn right onto Route 315 and drive 220 m to the trailhead, located on the right. There is an area to pull off the road and park.

Trailhead: 47°43'49.9" N, 65°45'23.9" W   **Waterfall:** 47°44'02.3" N, 65°45'06.6" W

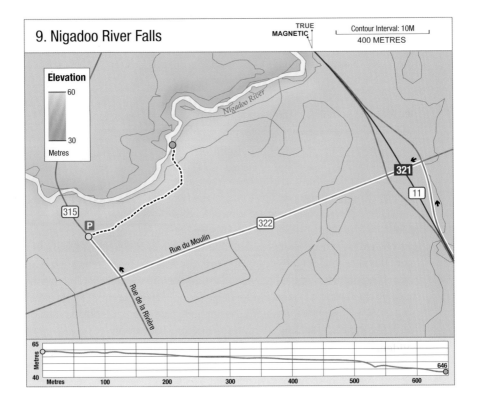

The hike: The property is part of the original land grant and homestead of the O'Connell family. They very graciously allow passage to see the waterfall. In spring, be on the lookout for wildflowers such as trilliums while following the old woods road through a mixed forest of hardwood and softwood. In autumn, the colours of New Brunswick are mesmerizing here. About 500 m along the trail, there is a Y junction. Stay to the left as the trail gently descends to the edge of the gorge. The coordinates provided lead downriver below the falls to one of the best viewing locations. Sit patiently and you might see a salmon struggling to leap the falls on its journey to its upriver spawning grounds.

L.W. Bailey's 1864 *Report on the mines and minerals of New Brunswick* describes the area as "a succession of romantic falls and rapids working their way backwards over the slate strata outcrops at Nickadoo [sic] Falls, running east and west injected with limestone, quartz, copper pyrites and lead." Little has changed over the years. The gorge is rich in geological structures with evidence of strata exposed by the wear of the river. The power of the river continues to cut a twisting ravine through the bedrock. Unfortunately, there are visitors who feel a need to leave litter behind and paint the rocks with useless graffiti.

10. Chute de la Rivière aux Ormes

TRUE
MAGNETIC

Contour Interval: 10M
1 KILOMETRE

Rivière aux Ormes

Chemin Lagacy

Chemin Alcida

Elevation

140

70

Metres

208
Metres
98

346

Metres | 100 | 200 | 300

10. Chute de la Rivière aux Ormes

Type: Cascade
Height: 3 m
Best season(s): Spring, fall
Access: Bushwhack
Source: Rivière aux Ormes
Distance (one way): 346 m
Difficulty: Moderate

Rating: 1
Hiking time: 30 minutes
Land ownership: Crown
Map: NTS 021P13 Pointe Verte
Nearby waterfall(s): Nigadoo River Falls
Cellphone coverage: Y

Finding the trailhead: Driving on Route 11 from Bathurst toward Dalhousie, take exit 326 for LaPlante. At the intersection, turn left and drive south to LaPlante. At the next intersection, continue straight for roughly 7.8 km along Chemin LaPlante to the junction with Chemin Alcida. Turn right and follow this road for about 6.7 km to the trailhead. The road is asphalt for some distance and then becomes a gravel woods road. The trailhead is in the middle of a clearcut.

Trailhead: 47°48'44.7" N, 65°51'10.6" W   **Waterfall:** 47°48'47.1" N, 65°51'26.0" W

The hike: From the clearcut, head in a westerly direction toward the woods and then a short bushwhack to the waterfalls. The falls are located in the remnants of the Appalachian Mountains before they slide into Chaleur Bay. The area surrounding the waterfall has been deforested in the past few years, causing feeder brooks to dry out quickly. The original trail leading from the opposite side of the waterfalls was destroyed by a clearcut.

In contrast to the day of my visit, when the waterfall had a scant amount of water, the acclaimed Acadian artist Réjean Roy captured the essence of this diminutive waterfall by making it much richer in his artistic rendering. Unlike an artist, who has the option to interpret and give the setting their personal touch, a photographer can only work with what is present at that visit. There is little doubt that the brook is seasonal in nature, and a return trip to this waterfall is required.

11. Antinouri Lake Brook Falls

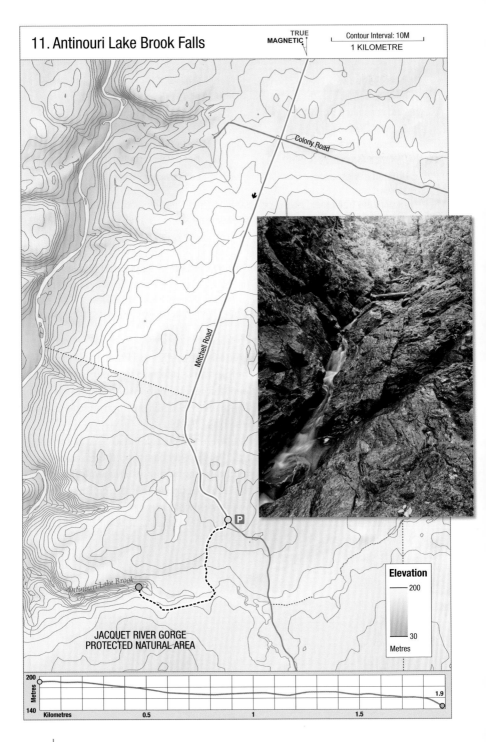

Colony Road

Mitchell Road

Antinouri Lake Brook

P

JACQUET RIVER GORGE
PROTECTED NATURAL AREA

Elevation
— 200

— 30
Metres

200
Metres
140
Kilometres   0.5   1   1.5   1.9

11. Antinouri Lake Brook Falls

Type: Slide
Height: 9 m
Best season(s): Spring, fall
Access: Trail, bushwhack
Source: Antinouri Lake Brook
Distance (one way): 1.9 km
Difficulty: Moderate to difficult

Rating: 2
Hiking time: 1 hour
Land ownership: Crown (Jacquet River Gorge Protected Natural Area)
Map: NTS 021O16 Charlo
Nearby waterfall(s): Nash Creek Falls
Cellphone coverage: N

Finding the trailhead: To visit Antinouri Falls, depart Route 11 near Jacquet River at exit 351. Turn right and drive north toward Chaleur Bay on Jacquet River Drive for about 500 m. Turn right onto Mitchell Road and drive for approximately 1.5 km to the Y junction. Take the road on the right and drive south past Mitchell Settlement. The road will change to gravel along the way. From the Y junction to the trailhead is just over 8 km.

Trailhead: 47°49'40.5" N, 66°00'24.8" W   **Waterfall:** 47°49'16.7" N, 66°01'10.6" W

The hike: The trailhead is the old logging road on the right. Follow it for roughly 1 km until reaching the brook. Once across the brook, continue 50 m or so and then cut right and begin to bushwhack, keeping the brook on the right. On the way down into the gulch, the rich aroma of cedar permeates the forest, filling one's senses with the richness of the earth. On my visit, the ravine was a kaleidoscope of every colour of green possible. It overwhelmed my senses! Unfortunately, on my visit to the fall in the unusually dry summer of 2020 the water level was very low.

The Jacquet River Gorge is a Protected Natural Area, and old-growth forest is prevalent along the steep banks. At the falls, the brook slides over an upper section of what would be the more dramatic of the two sections. In the lower section, the brook snakes down between the rocks on its journey to the Jacquet River.

12. Nash Creek Falls

Type: Tiered
Height: 3 m
Best season(s): Spring, fall
Access: Bushwhack
Source: Nash Creek and Lake Brook
Distance (one way): 400 m
Difficulty: Moderate to difficult

Rating: 2
Hiking time: 30 minutes
Land ownership: Private
Map: NTS 021O16 Charlo
Nearby waterfall(s): Cigar Falls, Antinouri Brook Falls
Cellphone coverage: Y

Finding the trailhead: Drive northwest from Bathurst on Route 11 toward the town of Dalhousie, looking for exit 357 to Nash Creek. Continue driving past the exit roughly 2.4 km to the trailhead coordinates, and park along the righthand shoulder of the highway. Immediately in front of the parking location, there is a deep ravine on the right.

Trailhead: 47°54'46.1" N, 66°06'33.3" W   **Waterfall:** 47°54'55.7" N, 66°06'33.5" W

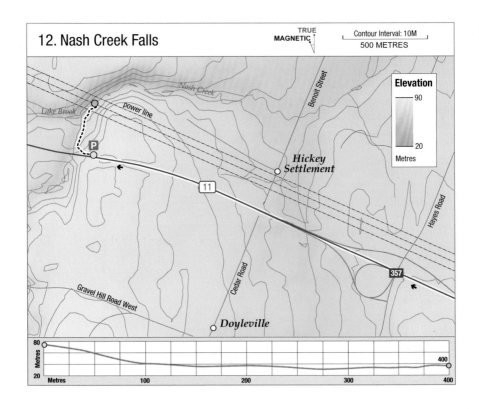

The hike: There is no marked trail from the roadside to this picturesque waterfall. From the road, head for the treeline and then slowly and carefully scramble down the boulder riprap that covers the culvert. Near Nash Creek, begin a bushwhack along the east side (righthand side) for approximately 300 m to the waterfall.

Nash Creek Falls, also known as Murchie Falls, is another of New Brunswick's roadside gems. Although there is no pool for swimming or diving, during warm summer days in years past, youngsters from the nearby village followed a well-trodden path to this relatively unknown waterfall and its ice-cold water to cool down in a peaceful location. Around 1900, the creek was dammed downstream, near the mouth, to generate power to run a shingle mill.

13. Secret Falls

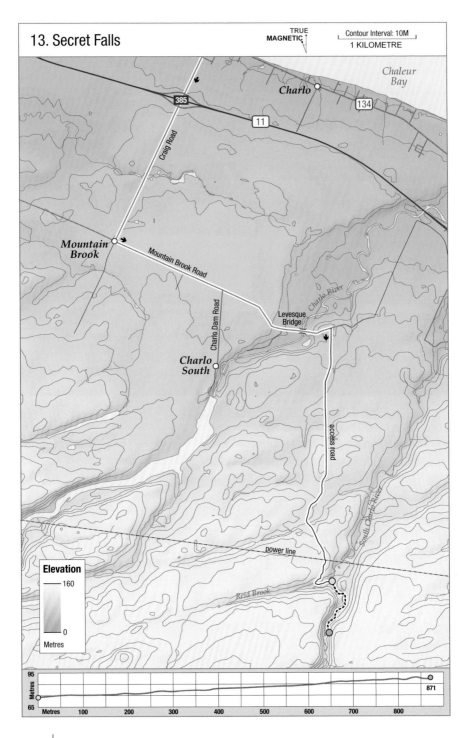

TRUE
MAGNETIC

Contour Interval: 10M
1 KILOMETRE

Chaleur Bay

Charlo

385

134

11

Craig Road

Mountain Brook

Mountain Brook Road

Charlo River

Levesque Bridge

Charlo Dam Road

Charlo South

access road

South Charlo River

power line

Reid Brook

Elevation
160

0
Metres

95

Metres

65   Metres   100   200   300   400   500   600   700   800

871

13. Secret Falls

Type: Tiered
Height: 2 m
Best season(s): Summer, fall
Access: River walk
Source: South Charlo River
Distance (one way): 871 m
Difficulty: Moderate

Rating: 3
Hiking time: 30 minutes
Land ownership: Crown
Map: NTS 021O16 Charlo
Nearby waterfall(s): Cigar Falls
Cellphone coverage: N

Finding the trailhead: From Chaleur Street (Route 134) in the village of Charlo, turn and drive out on Craig Road for 3 km to Mountain Brook Road. Turn left and drive roughly 3 km to the Charlo River Bridge #3, known locally as the Levesque Bridge. After crossing, drive to the access road on the right at 47°58'25.1" N, 66°19'30.4" W. Drive out this very good gravel road 3.7 km to the river. The last section, down to the river near a cluster of camps, can be pretty rough. If uncertain, park at the edge of the NB Power transmission lines and walk down the road to the river.

Trailhead: 47°56'40.1" N, 66°19'31.7" W **Waterfall:** 47°56'20.0" N, 66°19'34.1" W

The hike: There is no trail, only the river and a river walk that should not be attempted until mid-summer, when water levels are favourable. On a warm summer day, wading upstream to Secret Falls, also known as Eddy's Hole, is very enjoyable. Although the actual waterfall is diminutive, the basin and towering rock cliffs give the entire scene a supernatural appearance. It is one of the nicest waterfall settings that I have witnessed. The whole idea of walking in water on a return visit to Secret Falls has tugged at me since I last visited in 1975.

One would think that the waterfall might have been much higher due to the geological structure. I can only speculate that dynamite was used to release log jams, and over time, this activity increased the egress area for the river to exit into a large pool. Unfortunately, some people believe it is all right to use ATVs to drive up the river to enjoy the swimming. I just cannot wrap my head around this activity.

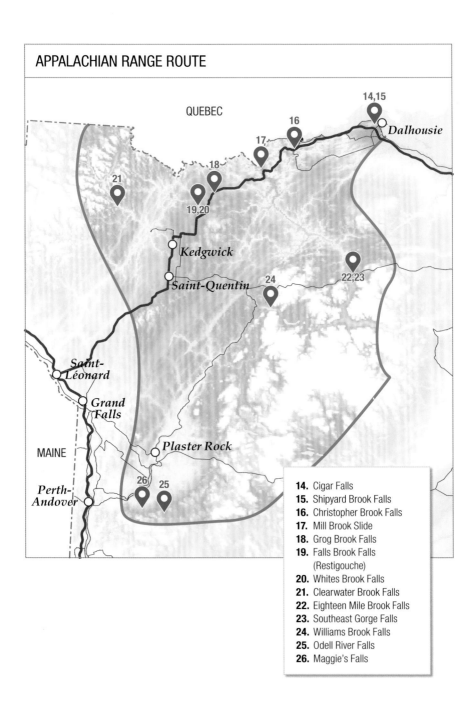

APPALACHIAN RANGE ROUTE

QUEBEC

Dalhousie

Kedgwick

Saint-Quentin

Saint-Léonard

Grand Falls

MAINE

Plaster Rock

Perth-Andover

14. Cigar Falls
15. Shipyard Brook Falls
16. Christopher Brook Falls
17. Mill Brook Slide
18. Grog Brook Falls
19. Falls Brook Falls (Restigouche)
20. Whites Brook Falls
21. Clearwater Brook Falls
22. Eighteen Mile Brook Falls
23. Southeast Gorge Falls
24. Williams Brook Falls
25. Odell River Falls
26. Maggie's Falls

Appalachian Range Route

The Province of New Brunswick's Appalachian Range Route follows the ancient mountain range southwest from the town of Dalhousie on Chaleur Bay to Perth-Andover, where it meets the River Valley Scenic Drive. Known as the Chaleur Uplands, the mountains stretch from the Tobique River valley across northern New Brunswick to Chaleur Bay, near Bathurst, and are predominately located along an ancient geological pressure ridge that had volcanic activity in the distant past. The crown jewel of the region is Mount Carleton Provincial Park, which offers the most sublime scenery in the province. Mount Carleton is the result of ancient volcanic action, along with Bald Peak and Sugarloaf Mountain near Campbellton. It is located at the dividing point of three major river systems: the Upsalquitch, which flows into the Restigouche; the Tobique, a tributary of the Wolastoq/Saint John; and the Nepisiguit, which empties into Chaleur Bay. This vast hinterland, which stretches in all directions with only a scattering of small communities, has changed little since it was described by naturalist William Francis Ganong at the turn of the nineteenth century.

Trilliums

The Appalachian route encompasses much of the Restigouche River valley, as well as the Tobique River valley. From Dalhousie, it follows the Restigouche River west before heading southwesterly to wind around lofty mountains through the settlements of Glencoe and Glen Levit. After crossing the Upsalquitch River at Robinsonville, the route climbs to the "top" of New Brunswick, an area with the highest sustained elevations in the province. Then, at Saint-Quentin, the route heads east toward Mount Carleton before curving southwest to follow the beautiful Tobique River for its entire length, providing an ample number of wonderful waterfalls to visit. It is easy to understand why this land was so important to the Wəlastəkwiyik and Mi'kmaq Peoples. There is no finer area for outdoor enthusiasts to bask in the beauty of our province.

26. Maggie's Falls

14. Cigar Falls

Type: Drop   **Rating:** 3

Height: 5 m   **Hiking time:** 20 minutes

Best season(s): Spring, fall   **Land ownership:** Private

Access: Trail, bushwhack   **Map:** NTS 022B01 Escuminac

Source: Cigar Falls Brook   **Nearby waterfall(s):** Shipyard Brook

Distance (one way): 569 m   Falls, Nash Creek Falls

Difficulty: Easy to moderate   **Cellphone coverage:** Y

Finding the trailhead: Driving northwest on Route 11, take exit 391 at Eel River Crossing. Drive straight to the stop sign, turn right onto Route 275, and head roughly 1.3 km toward the town of Dalhousie. At the junction with Sunset Drive, which requires a left turn on the top of a rise in the road, sometimes with oncoming traffic, turn left and drive 1.3 km to the trailhead. Park along the righthand shoulder of the roadway.

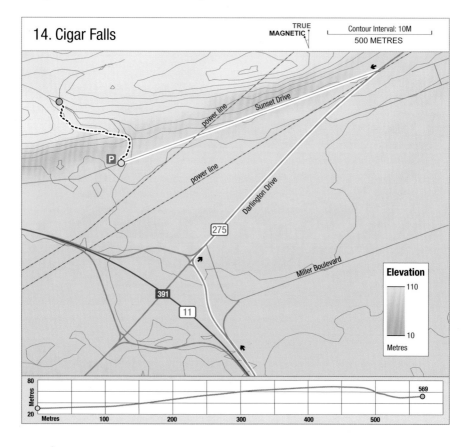

Trailhead: 48°02'33.2" N, 66°24'31.4" W **Waterfall:** 48°02'42.3" N, 66°24'45.9" W

The hike: Cigar Falls is tucked away in a lush secluded ravine on the outskirts of Dalhousie. The property belongs to the Reinsborough family, and they do not mind if nature enthusiasts visit. All they ask for in return is respect for their property. After parking, cross over the shallow ditch on the right and push through the brush to an open field. Hike along the edge of the field until reaching a farm road that leads up through the woods.

An autumn hike up the hill through the canopy of colours is just amazing and refreshing. When you emerge from the canopy at the top of the hill, cut right and head diagonally across the field into the woods. From here, it is a downhill bushwhack to the brook and a narrow waterfall gushing over the escarpment. This area of the ravine remains relatively wet and lush with vegetation throughout the year, especially during the spring and autumn. An alternate return to the trailhead is to hike down along the brook to an old dam that, at one time, provided water for the farm.

15. Shipyard Brook Falls

Type: Cascade	**Rating:** 1
Height: 3 m	**Hiking time:** 10 minutes
Best season(s): Spring	**Land ownership:** Crown
Access: Shore walk	**Map:** NTS 022B01 Escuminac
Source: Shipyard Brook	**Nearby waterfall(s):** Cigar Falls
Distance (one way): 203 m	**Cellphone coverage:** Y
Difficulty: Easy	

Finding the trailhead: In the town of Dalhousie, drive west on Queen Street toward the old ICI chemical plant. Just beyond the defunct railway tracks, there is a parking area on the right. The trailhead begins here.

Trailhead: 48°04'01.0" N, 66°23'50.0" W   **Waterfall:** 48°04'02.0" N, 66°23'45.1" W

The hike: This guide would not be complete without a waterfall from my home-town. From the parking area, walk down to the shore and then head east along the beach. The diminutive and relatively unknown Shipyard Brook Falls has the distinction of being the most northern of all New Brunswick waterfalls.

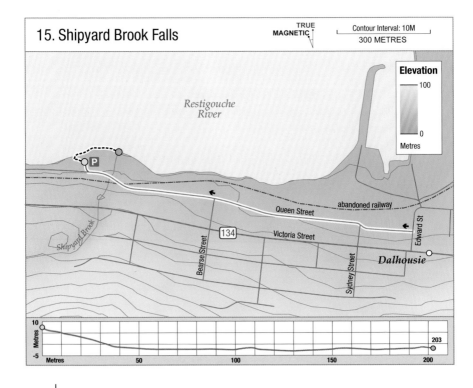

This brook is seasonal in nature. During the spring freshet and after a heavy rain, the quantity of water forcing its way toward the estuary gushes out from its rocky channel and strikes a rock outcrop at the beach that redirects the cascade up and over, making the falls.

Remember that you cannot enjoy Shipyard Brook Falls at high tide, so check the tide table before visiting. Otherwise, it may be a lost opportunity to photograph the waterfall, as well as a forced bushwhack along the edge of the shore when the tide comes in. There are remnants of a shipbuilding dock located relatively near to the brook. Over the years, harsh winter storms and heavy spring ice have all but reclaimed the timber and eroded much of the loose soil along the edge of the shore. Like most of the communities along the bay, Dalhousie was once a thriving shipbuilding and industrial centre, and flow from the brook was probably used to power a small sawmill.

16. Christopher Brook Falls

Type: Cascade
Height: 1.5 m
Best season(s): Summer, fall
Access: Trail
Source: Christopher Brook
Distance (one way): 29 m
Difficulty: Easy

Rating: 1
Hiking time: less than a minute
Land ownership: Crown
Map: NTS 021O15 Atholville
Nearby waterfall(s): Grog Brook Falls
Cellphone coverage: Y

Finding the trailhead: Christopher Brook Falls is located in Glencoe along Route 17, known locally as the Stewart Highway, between Campbellton and Saint-Léonard. The waterfall cannot be missed as it is very close to the highway. There is a small parking area near the waterfalls with a picnic table.

Trailhead: 47°57'21.1" N, 66°47'50.3" W   **Waterfall:** 47°57'21.7" N, 66°47'49.9" W

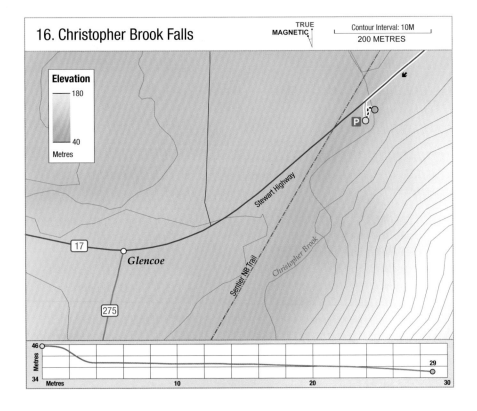

The hike: If a short break from driving is needed, then an energy-enriching stop at a roadside waterfall is the answer. Christopher Brook turns sharply and tumbles down 1.5 m into a small pool before continuing on its journey down to the Restigouche River. Across from the mouth of Christopher Brook is Quebec and the beginning of the Gaspé Peninsula.

Christopher Brook is named for James and Samuel Christopher, the original land grantees, who established a small community further up the brook from the falls. In the early 1800s, this area of the province was sparsely inhabited and only the hardiest of settlers made the deep valleys, known to the Scots as glens, into their new homes. Most were escaping famine or persecution and made the long journey to establish a sense of worth in a new country with the promise of freedom and land. Many Scots chose this area because of its resemblance to the highlands of their ancestral Scotland. Further up the valley are other small Scottish communities, such as Glen Levit and Robinsonville.

17. Mill Brook Slide

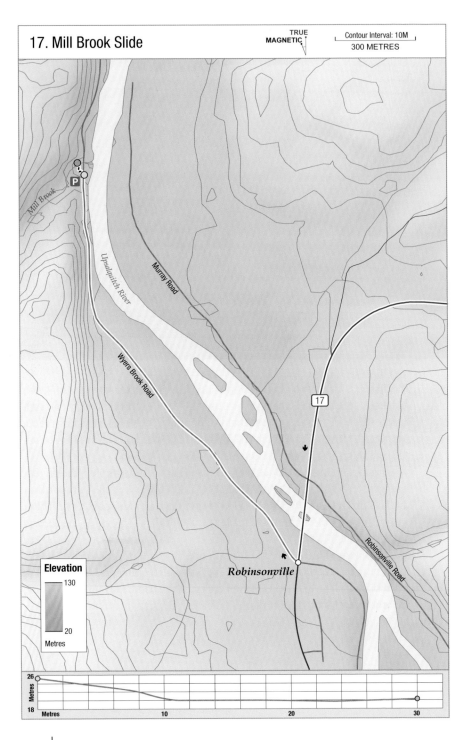

TRUE
MAGNETIC

Contour Interval: 10M
300 METRES

Mill Brook

P

Upsalquitch River

Murray Road

Wyers Brook Road

17

Robinsonville Road

Robinsonville

Elevation

130

20

Metres

17. Mill Brook Slide

Type: Slide
Height: 5 m
Best season(s): Spring, fall
Access: Trail
Source: Mill Brook
Distance (one way): 30 m
Difficulty: Easy

Rating: 1
Hiking time: 2 minutes
Land ownership: Private
Map: NTS 021O15 Atholville
Nearby waterfall(s): Christopher Brook Falls
Cellphone coverage: Y

Finding the trailhead: From Campbellton, head toward the village of Kedgwick on Route 17, known locally as the Stewart Highway. Just after crossing the Upsalquitch River in Robinsonville, turn right onto Wyers Brook Road and drive approximately 1.8 km on a paved and gravel road to the trailhead. Stop and park alongside the road.

Trailhead: 47°53'10.5" N, 66°57'30.1" W
Waterfall: 47°53'10.8" N, 66°57'30.5" W

The hike: Look for the short trail on the upper side of the road. Follow it down to a wooden culvert and a small clearing to see this roadside waterfall. The finest time to photograph Mill Brook is when the slide is shrouded with embracing autumn colours. The brook is cradled by Squaw Cap Mountain and the other mountains that make up the Appalachian range in New Brunswick. Scattered throughout the region are numerous diminutive brooks that twist and turn on their journey through these lofty mountains, all the while chiseling deep, narrow valleys. It is by far one of the most picturesque areas of our province.

Mill Brook is within the property of the Camp Harmony Angling Club, located further down Wyers Brook Road. This famous salmon fishing camp at the confluence of the Upsalquitch and Restigouche commands a spectacular view over both rivers. The camp has hosted many well-known American socialites and millionaires over its hundred-year existence. The sprawling log building was designed in the 1890s by renowned architect Stanford White for owner Dean Sage, a New York multimillionaire.

18. Grog Brook Falls

TRUE
MAGNETIC

Contour Interval: 10M
1 KILOMETRE

Elevation

340

220

Metres

17 Stewart Highway

Menneval

Grog Brook

bonus falls

International Appalachian Trail

P

270

Metres

220

Kilometres | 1 | 2 | 3

18. Grog Brook Falls

Type: Cascade
Height: 3 m
Best season(s): Spring, fall
Access: Trail
Source: Grog Brook
Distance (one way): 3 km
Difficulty: Easy

Rating: 2
Hiking time: 1 hour
Land ownership: Crown
Map: NTS 021O14 Menneval
Nearby waterfall(s): Mill Brook Slide
Cellphone coverage: N

Finding the trailhead: From Campbellton, head west toward the village of Kedgwick on Route 17, known locally as the Stewart Highway. In the roadside community of Menneval, look for a gravel road leading into the woods on the left at 47°47'56.1" N, 67°11'21.9" W. Drive in to the multiuse trail and turn left. Drive across the bridge to a gravel pit on the right and park. From the pit, hike southeasterly along the trail to the waterfalls.

Trailhead: 47°47'52.1" N, 67°11'06.8" W   **Waterfall:** 47°48'17.4" N, 67°08'50.7" W

The hike: The old railway running northeast from Saint-Léonard, near the Maine border, to Matapédia, Quebec, followed the gradual upstream slope of the Grand River eastward to the headwaters, across the mountains, and then gradually along the downstream decline of Grog Brook toward the Upsalquitch River. The railbed is now part of the International Appalachian Trail through northern New Brunswick, connecting the state of Maine in the west to the province of Quebec in the east. The surrounding hills provide this section of the trail with its most spectacular views.

Cradled within these lofty mountains, which make up part of the Appalachian range, Grog Brook twists and turns on its journey, all the while carving a deep and narrow valley. The hike is very pleasurable, especially during the short autumn interlude before the onset of winter. In this, one of the most picturesque areas of our province, temperatures begin a gradual descent earlier than in southern New Brunswick. The trail is underutilized by hikers and is predominately used by ATV and snowmobile enthusiasts.

Bonus fall(s): On the hike to the waterfall, check out the smaller falls at 47°48'04.7" N, 67°09'29.1" W. It can be seen from the trail.

19. Falls Brook Falls (Restigouche)

Type: Tiered
Height: 10 m
Best season(s): Summer, fall
Access: Trail, bushwhack
Source: Falls Brook (Restigouche)
Distance (one way): 420 m
Difficulty: Moderate

Rating: 5
Hiking time: 30 minutes
Land ownership: Crown
Map: NTS 021O14 Menneval
Nearby waterfall(s): Grog Brook Falls, Whites Brook Falls
Cellphone coverage: N

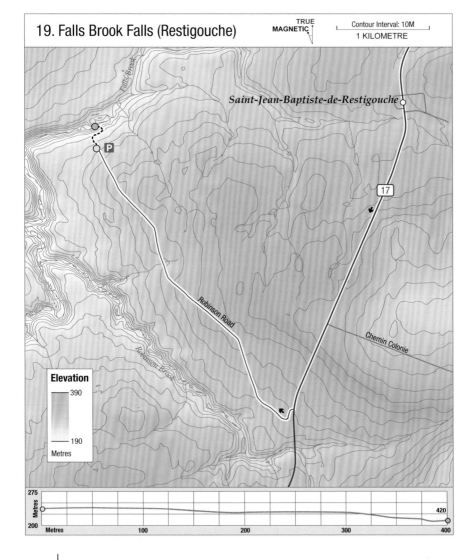

19. Falls Brook Falls (Restigouche)

19. Falls Brook Falls (Restigouche)

Finding the trailhead: From Campbellton, head west toward the village of Kedgwick on Route 17, known locally as the Stewart Highway. Roughly 3.5 km beyond the village of Saint-Jean-Baptiste-de-Restigouche, look for the road on the right at 47°44'14.2" N, 67°13'38.6" W. Locally known as Robinson Road, it is one of the many hauling roads for logging operations along the Restigouche River. Drive out the gravel road approximately 3.8 km to the trailhead. The road has a solid base with no wet or grown-in areas to contend with. On the drive into the trailhead, there is a chance of seeing moose, deer, or bears foraging. There is little doubt that logging operations change the landscape, and this transformation is prevalent in western Restigouche County.

Trailhead: 47°45'43.5" N, 67°15'19.7" W
Waterfall: 47°45'51.1" N, 67°15'20.2" W

The hike: From the trailhead, begin hiking straight down the cut road and push through a short section of brush to a secondary trail. Continue hiking down and then up along the brook for roughly 100 m. Look for a space to undertake a short bushwhack to the top of the waterfalls. It is better to approach from the top, as the cliffs are rather steep along the ravine below the falls. Near the cascade, there is a rough trail leading down to the base.

It is at this fall that the brook begins its wild journey, dropping from the highlands into the Restigouche River. The brook is aptly named as there are numerous ledges and two additional waterfalls further downstream to explore. Falls Brook Falls is what I call "yummy." It is very easy to remain for hours to photograph this natural and beautiful waterfall setting. It is a location that warrants many return trips.

20. Whites Brook Falls

Type: Drop, tiered
Height: 20 m
Best season(s): Summer, fall
Access: Trail
Source: Whites Brook
Distance (one way): 4.4 km
Difficulty: Moderate to difficult

Rating: 5
Hiking time: 2 hours
Land ownership: Crown, private
Map: NTS 021O14 Menneval
Nearby waterfall(s): Falls Brook Falls, Grog Brook Falls
Cellphone coverage: N

Finding the trailhead: From Campbellton, head west toward the village of Kedgwick on Route 17, known locally as the Stewart Highway. Roughly 5.7 km beyond the village of Saint-Jean-Baptiste-de-Restigouche, look for a logging road and the trailhead on the right. Vehicle access to the road is blocked. The property near the road is private, although the waterfall is located on Crown land.

Trailhead: 47°43'22.3" N, 67°14'33.5" W **Waterfall:** 47°44'30.2" N, 67°16'14.6" W

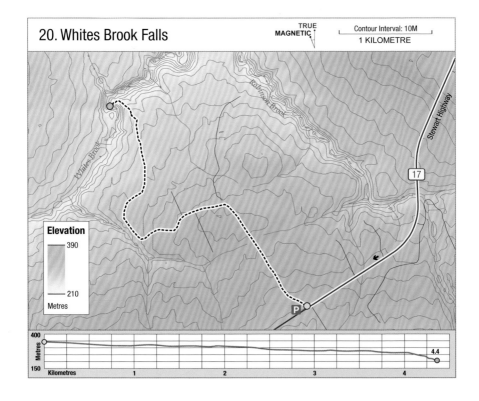

The hike: Park alongside the highway and begin walking out on the road, roughly 4.5 km, to one of the best waterfalls in Restigouche County, if not all of New Brunswick. It is a very good logging road to walk along. Near the waterfall, the logging road changes to an ATV trail and, eventually, just a walking path. Near this section, there are the remnants of a structure that has been removed or destroyed. The owner of the private road has installed a large rope barricade to maintain a buffer between the trail and the sheer cliffs that surround the waterfall as it drops 25 m to the pool at the base.

This waterfall is in one of the wildest natural settings I have witnessed and photographed in this province. At one time, New Brunswick's natural resources department studied the merits of developing the area around the waterfall as an ecosite destination but decided in favour of other locations. On nearby Crown land, there is an old logging road that may be upgraded as an ATV trail to the waterfall.

21. Clearwater Brook Falls

TRUE
MAGNETIC

Contour Interval: 10M
300 METRES

Elevation
270
150
Metres

Clearwater Brook

Kedgwick River

main logging road

P

South Branch Clearwater Brook

183
Metres
168
163
Metres   50   100   150

21. Clearwater Brook Falls

Type: Cascade
Height: 10 m
Best season(s): Spring, fall
Access: Bushwhack
Source: South Branch Clearwater Brook
Distance (one way): 163 m
Difficulty: Moderate

Rating: 2
Hiking time: 20 minutes
Land ownership: Crown
Map: NTS 021O12 Gounamitz River
Nearby waterfall(s): Whites Brook Falls
Cellphone coverage: N

Finding the trailhead: Drive east toward Kedgwick on Route 17 from Saint-Quentin and take the exit for Route 265 to Kedgwick River. Continue through the hamlet and over the bridge spanning the Little Main Restigouche River. Stay right and follow the main logging road toward Rapids Depot for roughly a distance of 19 km until you see the sign for Clearwater Lake at 47°44'05.8" N, 67°39'12.6" W. Turn left and drive a distance of nearly 900 m to the first brook that crosses under this road. Park along the righthand side near the bridge.

Trailhead: 47°44'09.4" N, 67°39'55.2" W **Waterfall:** 47°44'13.9" N, 67°39'58.4" W

The hike: Bushwhack into the woods 100 m down along the west side of the brook to the waterfall. There is no questioning how this brook received its appropriate name; the South Branch Clearwater Brook is "gin clear," with a slight tint of emerald.

The sparkling Clearwater Brook Falls is located in the Appalachian Mountains, which rise to more than 500 m in this wilderness section of Restigouche County. You could drive for an entire day without encountering another person; you are more likely to stumble across a moose, foraging in one of the many bogans, or see the dust from a bear skedaddling across a clearcut. This is also timber country. The area has been harvested since the late 1800s, and during the early days of logging, many of its waterways were filled with timber floating down to the nearest sawmills.

22. Eighteen Mile Brook Falls

Type: Tiered
Height: 8 m
Best season(s): Summer, fall
Access: River walk, bushwhack
Source: Eighteen Mile Brook
Distance (one way): 767 m
Difficulty: Difficult

Rating: 3
Hiking time: 40 minutes
Land ownership: Crown
Map: NTS 021O09 Camel Back Mountain
Nearby waterfall(s): Southeast Gorge Falls
Cellphone coverage: N

Finding the trailhead: From either Bathurst in the east or Saint-Quentin in the west, drive out Route 180 to the trailhead coordinates and park alongside the road, away from the guardrails. Constructed in the late 1970s, Route 180 (known locally as the Road to Resources) provides easy access to the mineral and forest resources of northern New Brunswick. Note that this is a wilderness area, so be well-prepared before heading out on this excursion. It is recommended that you tackle this waterfall and route during the summer and autumn, when water levels are lower.

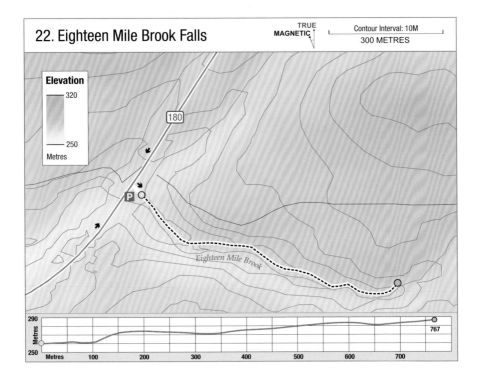

Trailhead: 47°32'56.2" N, 66°29'01.2" W **Waterfall:** 47°32'48.6" N, 66°28'29.2" W

The hike: From the road, scramble down the embankment and bushwhack along the east side of the brook while heading up to the falls. Be very careful in the area near the waterfall where the ravine becomes rather steep. The waterfall is both engaging and spectacular.

With meager beginnings in the narrow ravines of Camel Back Mountain and Mount Jack, Eighteen Mile Brook derives its name from the fact that it conjoins with the Southeast Upsalquitch River eighteen miles (twenty-four kilometres) upriver from the Upsalquitch Forks. This naming-by-number convention made it easier for lumbermen at the turn of the twentieth century to identify the brook where they were working. The measurement is not the same as the length of the watercourse; it is a means of locating any feature, such as an island or tributary, relative to its distance from the river mouth when measured along the course of the river.

23. Southeast Gorge Falls

Type: Drop
Height: 3 m
Best season(s): Summer, fall
Access: Bushwhack
Source: Southeast Upsalquitch River
Distance (one way): 579 m
Difficulty: Moderate to difficult

Rating: 3
Hiking time: 30 minutes
Land ownership: Crown
Map: NTS 021O10 Upsalquitch Forks
Nearby waterfall(s): Eighteen Mile Brook Falls
Cellphone coverage: N

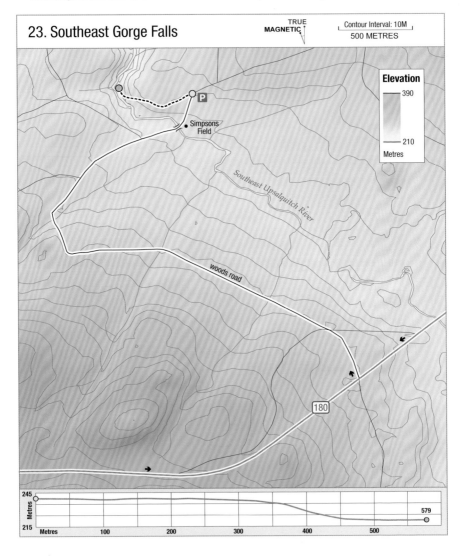

Finding the trailhead: Drive Route 180 (the Road to Resources) west from Bathurst or east from Saint-Quentin and turn north at coordinates 47°32'11.3" N, 66°30'35.2" W. The gravel woods road leads down the west side of the Southeast Upsalquitch River and is part of the Ramsay Portage, historically used to bypass the gorge. Drive roughly 3.8 km and park at the trailhead waypoint. Just before the trailhead, there is a cabin on the left and a logging bridge spanning the river. This is a wilderness area, so be well-prepared for this excursion.

Trailhead: 47°33'12.2" N, 66°31'27.8" W **Waterfall:** 47°33'13.5" N, 66°31'52.5" W

The hike: There is no defined path, so bushwhack along the old logging road on the left, following the contour of the river. You can hear the water as it leads to the series of four waterfalls in this part of the river, and it is here that the height and sheerness of the fissure is exposed. The western side provides a rampart of sorts, curling the river back to the east where a large pool is produced before it continues down through the fault in a series of waterfalls to crash against sheer walls of rock. This is a wondrous place. The height of the fault blocks the sun from entering the gorge, and it is safe to surmise that the summer sun reaches into the abyss only momentarily before returning it back into shadow; in mid-winter the area would remain in shadow all day.

The Upsalquitch has two main branches. The gentler Northwest Upsalquitch River hugs the deep valleys of the Appalachian Mountains. The Southeast Upsalquitch River cuts northerly along a geological fault line through the mountains to form an impressive river gorge. In this narrow, twisting rift, the sound of water crashing against the bedrock is thunderous.

24. Williams Brook Falls

TRUE
MAGNETIC

Contour Interval: 10M

400 METRES

MOUNT CARLETON
PROVINCIAL PARK

Elevation

310

250

Metres

P

*Nictau
Lake*

Williams Brook
Campground

Williams Brook

310
Metres
250 | Metres | 50 | 100 | 150 | 200 | 243

24. Williams Brook Falls

Type: Tiered
Height: 3 m
Best season(s): Spring, summer, fall
Access: Trail
Source: Williams Brook
Distance (one way): 243 m
Difficulty: Easy

Rating: 3
Hiking time: 10 minutes
Land ownership: Crown (Mount Carleton Provincial Park, fees apply)
Map: NTS 021O07 Nepisiguit Lakes
Nearby waterfall(s): Odell River Falls
Cellphone coverage: N

Finding the trailhead: Williams Brook Falls is located in Mount Carleton Provincial Park. From the park entrance, drive roughly 1.3 km and turn left. From this turnoff, continue an additional 5 km, passing the Armstrong Brook and Williams Brook campgrounds. The trailhead for the waterfall is on the righthand side of the road and is identified.

Trailhead: 47°25'35.6" N, 66°53'02.0" W   **Waterfall:** 47°25'34.1" N, 66°52'53.2" W

The hike: This wheelchair-accessible trail and boardwalk wind through the forest for approximately 250 m until reaching a wooden bridge over the brook, just above the falls. There are some great viewpoints from here, as well as from a lookout located below the falls. The sound of the brook, tumbling over mossy mounds and glistening tree roots, is harmonious with the beautiful scene of hardwood and softwood trees surrounding the waterfall. Directly across from and facing the falls is a smooth rock surface that causes the brook to abruptly change direction.

Mount Carleton Provincial Park is a beautiful, unspoiled wilderness of large crystalline lakes, rounded mountains, and abundant wildlife. The central feature is Mount Carleton — at 817 m, the highest point in the Maritime provinces. These mountains are part of the Appalachians, which extend from the southeastern United States north to New Brunswick and into Quebec.

25. Odell River Falls

Type: Drop
Height: 13 m
Best season(s): Summer, fall
Access: Bushwhack, trail
Source: Odell River
Distance (one way): 1.4 km
Difficulty: Moderate to difficult

Rating: 4
Hiking time: 1 hour
Land ownership: Crown (Acadian Timber lease, fees apply)
Map: NTS 021J14 Plaster Rock
Nearby waterfall(s): Williams Brook Falls
Cellphone coverage: N

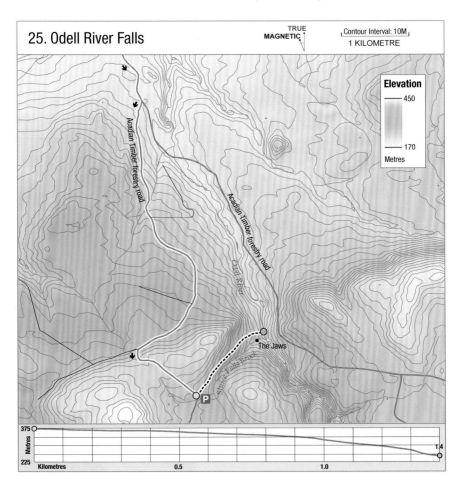

Note: Before venturing to the Tobique River to see Odell River Falls, contact the Acadian Timber Corp. (www.acadiantimber.com) to determine where Recreation Day Passes are sold. A pass is required to have access to their forestry roads.

Finding the trailhead: From Perth-Andover, drive northeast on Route 109 to Arthurette and continue up the south side of the Tobique River on Route 390 toward the small hamlet of Odell. Near where the Odell River meets the Tobique River is the Acadian Timber Corp. forestry road at 46°48'42.6" N, 67°26'03.8" W. Drive to the gate and use the phone provided to contact Acadian Timber for access, giving the required name, pass number, and vehicle license number. The logging road is well maintained. Drive for roughly 7 km until reaching a Y junction in the road. Stay to the right and drive a further 5.5 km to the trailhead.

Trailhead: 46°43'41.3" N, 67°21'52.4" W   **Waterfall:** 46°44'06.8" N, 67°21'08.2" W

The hike: The trail from the logging road has begun to grow over where it descends into the Odell River valley and gradually increases in pitch. Near the bottom is a Y junction in the trail. Take the righthand trail, which is steep but manageable. The forested area adjacent to the river is undisturbed, mainly due to the steepness of the hillsides flanking the river. Near the waterfall, there is a series of ledges that provide an excellent vantage point. At 13 m high, the falls drop straight into a large basin, sending forth a roar that reverberates along the rock walls and up into the forest. Caution is required due to the amount of moisture along the moss-laden ledges.

Bonus fall(s): An added feature is The Jaws. Go back up the trail to 46°44'8.3" N, 67°21'09.4" W and follow a short trail down to Sluice Falls Brook. The brook has cut a narrow crevice through the ridge above, forming a 5 m waterfall.

26. Maggie's Falls

Type: Drop, tiered
Height: Various
Best season(s): Spring, summer, fall
Access: Trail
Source: Odellach River
Distance (one way): 1.14 km
Difficulty: Easy

Rating: 5
Hiking time: 30 minutes
Land ownership: Private
Map: NTS 021J11 Juniper
Nearby waterfall(s): Odell River Falls, Four Falls
Cellphone coverage: N

Finding the trailhead: From Perth-Andover, drive on Route 109 toward Arthurette and Plaster Rock. As you near Arthurette, look for Birch Ridge Road on the right. Head south into the hills along Birch Ridge Road for a distance of 6 km until the road reaches four corners with Birch Ridge Crossing Road on the right and a private road on the left. At the four corners, park alongside the main road and walk in the private road and through the gate with a sign that states walking is permitted. The trail is the road used by the property owners, who have a camp near the falls. Please treat the property with respect.

26. Maggie's Falls

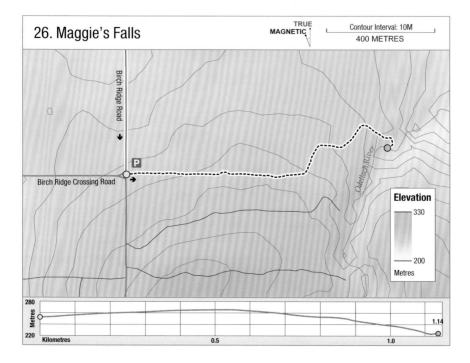

Trailhead: 46°44'16.1" N, 67°28'25.4" W **Waterfall:** 46°44'19.7" N, 67°27'39.9" W

The hike: It takes roughly fifteen minutes to reach Maggie's Falls, which are situated in very arresting surroundings. The Odellach River has notched a ravine almost a kilometre long into the bedrock, producing a multifaceted series of beautiful cascades that twist and turn on their journey to the Tobique River. The rock ledges that form each of the several falls lend them a unique appearance; follow the trails and you'll find lots of different waterfalls. There is an abundance of large pine trees in the area.

According to local lore, a woman named Maggie (Margaret) Grey lived by the falls and charged children a fee to visit the area and swim. Regardless of the truth of the tale, it feels both special and magical, making it understandable why so many people visit from far and wide. Take some time to enjoy this little paradise.

26. Maggie's Falls

RIVER VALLEY SCENIC DRIVE

QUEBEC

Dalhousie

27,28

Kedgwick

29

Saint-Quentin

Edmundston

Saint-Léonard

Grand Falls

30

Plaster Rock

31

Perth-Andover

32

MAINE

Doaktown

33,34,35

40,41

Woodstock

36,37

38,39

Fredericton

42,43,44

45,46,47

51

Sussex

54

48,49

50,52,53

St. Stephen

Saint John

Bay of Fundy

CANADA - USA

27. Falls Brook Falls
    (Madawaska)
28. Gagne Falls
29. Chute de la Quisibis
30. Four Falls
31. Craig Falls
32. Briggs Millpond Falls
33. Jennings Falls
34. Millseat Falls
35. Gibson Creek Falls
36. Hays Falls
37. Eel River Falls

38. Sullivan Creek Falls
39. Big Falls (Shogomoc)
40. Coac Stream Falls
41. Mactaquac Stream Falls
42. Howland Falls
43. Lower Joslin Creek Falls
44. Split Rock Falls
45. Pete Brook Falls
46. Carrow Brook Falls
47. Scribner Brook Falls
48. Raggedy Ass Falls
49. Hubble Brook Falls
50. Sand Brook Falls
51. Mooneys Ridge Falls
52. Welsford Falls
53. Cunningham Creek Falls
54. Wyman Mills Falls

River Valley Scenic Drive

One of eastern Canada's longest rivers, the Wolastoq/Saint John River also has one of the largest drainage basins on the east coast at about 55,000 sq km, or an area the size of Lake Huron. It is within this basin that the River Valley Scenic Drive is found. It is said that the history of human civilization has been determined and controlled by its great rivers. Known as the Rhine of North America, the Wolastoq/Saint John River was for many centuries New Brunswick's primary communication and transportation route. Beginning at the Quebec border, the tourism route follows the Madawaska River valley until crossing over to follow the Wolastoq/Saint John River at Edmundston for its province-long dance south. The route runs through a dramatic landscape of mountain ridges and deep valleys and, in doing so, across several geological formations and some of the most fertile land in our province on its journey to the Bay of Fundy.

At first, the Scenic Drive follows the valley through the Appalachian Mountains, where it is flanked by rolling hills and waterfalls nestled in deep valleys. After Edmundston, the valley widens before attaining any height until it reaches Grand Falls, the home of the largest waterfall in the Maritime provinces. After the river cuts through this magnificent gorge, the mountains rise up. From this point south to Fredericton, the valley is etched deep by numerous watercourses with waterfalls that drop fifteen to eighteen metres, such as Rapide de Femme, Hays

40. Coac Stream Falls

48. Raggedy Ass Falls

Falls, and Coac Stream Falls. Below the capital city, the valley becomes a broad lowland, dominated by the province's largest lake, Grand Lake, and various wetlands that are home to migrating Canada geese and a multitude of duck species.

After the village of Gagetown, the character of the river changes yet again as the valley narrows until its exodus into the Bay of Fundy in the port city of Saint John. To the west of the river, the Juvenile Hills and the Nerepis Hills provide several outstanding waterfalls. Of note are Raggedy Ass Falls and Welsford Falls. One unusual feature of the Wolastoq/Saint John River is the narrow channel through which the river squeezes into the Bay of Fundy. Combined with the extreme tides of the Bay, this forces the river to reverse direction and flow upriver on every rising tide. The river once had at least four outlets, but geological changes in the earth's crust forced the land upward, closing all except what is now known as the Reversing Falls.

28. Gagne Falls

27. Falls Brook Falls (Madawaska)

TRUE
MAGNETIC

Contour Interval: 10M
1 KILOMETRE

QUEBEC

Falls Brook

Rivière Iroquois

Falls Brook Road

Petite rivière Iroquois

Chemin Rang 6

Chemin Iroquois

Ruisseau Richard

Chemin Roussel et Martin

Elevation
— 410

— 210
Metres

285
Metres
265 | 460

Metres | 100 | 200 | 300 | 400

27. Falls Brook Falls (Madawaska)

Type: Drop
Height: 10 m
Best season(s): Summer, fall
Access: Trail
Source: Falls Brook
Distance (one way): 460 m
Difficulty: Easy

Rating: 4
Hiking time: 20 minutes
Land ownership: Crown
Map: NTS 021N09 Grandmaison
Nearby waterfall(s): Gagne Falls
Cellphone coverage: N

Finding the trailhead: Driving north on Route 2 (TCH), take exit 16 at Edmundston, turn left at the intersection, and drive downhill to rue Victoria. At the intersection, turn right and drive north to the village of Saint-Jacques. Stay right at the stop where three roads meet and take Chemin St. Joseph. This road leads over the mountain and down into the Rivière Iroquois valley and the community of Moulin-Morneault. Continue and turn left onto Chemin Iroquois immediately after crossing the bridge over the Rivière Iroquois. The asphalt eventually turns into a well-maintained gravel road that changes name to Falls Brook Road. The trailhead is located on the right, just past a cluster of camps and the 6 km marker before the small bridge over Falls Brook. It is approximately 17 km from the turn at Chemin St. Joseph.

Trailhead: 47°35'06.8" N, 68°22'16.5" W   **Waterfall:** 47°35'17.7" N, 68°22'4.7" W

The hike: Walking along the maintained trail leading to the falls, the visitor is serenaded by Falls Brook as it tumbles through this mountainous region. Here in the Appalachian Mountains, with their lofty summits and deep valleys, is Madawaska County's version of Falls Brook Falls. This hidden gem, tucked away next to the border with Quebec, is well worth the time and effort of a long drive. Falls Brook flows in a southwesterly direction as it etches a path to the Rivière Iroquois, which, in turn, follows the contours of a broad valley to empty into the mighty Wolastoq/Saint John River.

With a 10 m plunge, this is a very fine and easily accessible waterfall. There are smooth flat rocks at the base of the falls and, in season, plenty of purple trilliums to guide the enthusiast along the path.

28. Gagne Falls

Type: Drop
Height: 7 m
Best season(s): Summer, fall
Access: Trail
Source: Gagne Brook
Distance (one way): 173 m
Difficulty: Easy

Rating: 4
Hiking time: 10 minutes
Land ownership: Crown
Map: NTS 021N09 Grandmaison
Nearby waterfall(s): Falls Brook Falls, Chute de la Quisibis
Cellphone coverage: N

Finding the trailhead: Take exit 16 from Route 2 (TCH) at Edmundston, turn left at the intersection, and drive downhill to rue Victoria. At the intersection, turn right and drive north. Turn right again on rue Boucher and drive uphill through a residential area, eventually crossing the Rivière Iroquois. The road name changes to Chemin Deuxième-Sault. Continue until a Y junction at 47°27'23.9" N, 68°14'05.6" W and stay left on Chemin Rang 8 until rue Ruisseau à Lunts on the right. From this point, there is a well-maintained gravel road, except for the 2.5 km leading from the main logging road to the trailhead. Remain on the main logging road, staying to the right at all Y junctions except the last two. Take the left at 47°35'13.1" N, 68°14'05.2" W and take a left at the next main junction just after crossing Gagne Brook at 47°36'49.2" N, 68°15'12.1" W. The road on the left leads uphill to the trailhead, which is 23.5 km distant from the turn onto Chemin Rang 8.

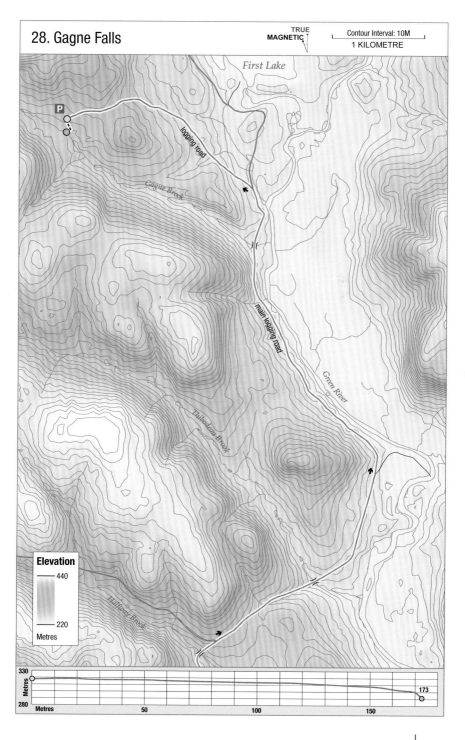

Trailhead: 47°37'11.1" N, 68°16'48.1" W
Waterfall: 47°37'7.3" N, 68°16'48.2" W

The hike: Located in the eastern wilderness of
Madawaska County, the eye-catching waterfall on
Gagne Brook is a prize well worth the effort for any
waterfall enthusiast. The hike begins on an ATV
trail, then a footpath descends to the base of the
falls. Gagne is a waterfall postcard waiting to be
photographed. Nestled in a ravine of rich green
foliage and concealed by a canopy of hardwoods,
the brook crashes over a sheer rock face, plunging
into a small, shallow pool and cool, moist ravine.
Located somewhere in this waterfall is a Garmin
GPS I lost a decade ago.

28. Gagne Falls

29. Chute de la Quisibis

TRUE
MAGNETIC

Contour Interval: 10M
1 KILOMETRE

Elevation

480

190

Metres

Beardsley Brook

Hunter Brook

Rivière Quisibis

P

Chemin Roy

Montagne-des-Roy

Chemin Clément Roy

Chemin Vaillancourt

Chemin Roy

Chemin Rivière Quisibis

Montagne-de-la-Croix

300
Metres
240

Metres 100 200 300 400 500 600 700 800

807

29. Chute de la Quisibis

Type: Drop
Height: 14 m
Best season(s): Summer, fall
Access: Trail
Source: Rivière Quisibis
Distance (one way): 807 m
Difficulty: Easy to moderate

Rating: 4
Hiking time: 20 minutes
Land ownership: Crown
Map: NTS 021O05 Grand River
Nearby waterfall(s): Falls Brook Falls, Gagne Falls
Cellphone coverage: No

Finding the trailhead: Getting to the Chute de la Quisibis takes a bit of driving. As with much of New Brunswick, the area is a maze of logging roads, some of which are no longer in use and can easily lead people unfamiliar with the area astray. Drive north toward Edmundston on Route 2 (TCH) and take exit 32 to Rivière-Verte. At the intersection with Davis Road, turn left and drive roughly 300 m. Turn right, crossing the river and following Chemin Rivière Quisibis. Look for the sign for Chute de la Quisibis on chemin Roy at 47°21'22.8" N, 68°02'19.9" W. Turn left, drive out this road, and stay to the left where the road turns to gravel. The access road is rough for 10.5 km and requires a vehicle with appropriate clearance. Stay right at the Y junction at 47°23'57.8" N, 68°01'10.6" W and turn right at 47°25'38.4" N, 68°00'20.7" W. Drive out this road and turn left at 47°25'16.5" N, 68°00'15.7" W, driving until reaching the trailhead.

Trailhead: 47°24'59.7" N, 68°00'00.6" W **Waterfall:** 47°24'44.4" N, 67°59'42.4" W

The hike: From the trailhead, it is a ten-minute walk on an ATV trail to the wilderness camping and picnic site at the top of the falls. A path just before the campsite leads through the woods to a rope assist for the climb down to the pool below the falls. The forest surrounding Quisibis Mountain has been cut, leaving rich scents of cedar and balsam fir along with a scarred landscape. Chute de la Quisibis has carved out an impressive ravine, a wonderful natural site formed by the eternal churning of the river. Located in the shadow of the mountain, this waterfall is one of the crown jewels of the Madawaska County wilderness.

30. Four Falls

Type: Tiered
Height: Various
Best season(s): Summer, fall
Access: Trail
Source: Four Falls Stream
Distance (one way): 205 m
Difficulty: Easy

Rating: 4
Hiking time: 10 minutes
Land ownership: Crown
Map: NTS 021J13 Aroostook
Nearby waterfall(s): Maggie's Falls
Cellphone coverage: Y

Finding the trailhead: Driving north on Route 2 (TCH), take exit 107 to Aroostook and follow the exit to the junction with Route 130. Turn left and drive along the Aroostook River to the exit for route 130 North. Follow route 130 across the old TCH Bridge to Four Falls and turn left onto Brown Road. Within roughly 300 m, the road crosses a cement bridge over the stream and waterfalls with the trailhead just beyond.

Trailhead: 46°49'27.5" N, 67°44'20.4" W   **Waterfall:** 46°49'24.2" N, 67°44'14.9" W

The hike: From the trailhead, follow the woods road down along the west side of the stream to the best observing area, just below the third cascade. As one would surmise, there are four major drops, along with a number of smaller falls. A thick canopy of mature trees provides an amazing wilderness feeling, even with the close proximity to the highway and nearby homes. The falls start above the road, where there was once a dam, and end with a final drop near the Aroostook River. The exposed bedrock along this steep ravine points upstream at acute angles. Adding to this wild scene is the roar of the water as it careens over and around large boulders.

The Aroostook War (1838-39) occurred in this area over the location of the boundary between Britain and the emerging country of the United States. The Americans laid claim to the area, and it was not until the Webster-Ashburton Treaty of 1842 that the area was judged to be British territory.

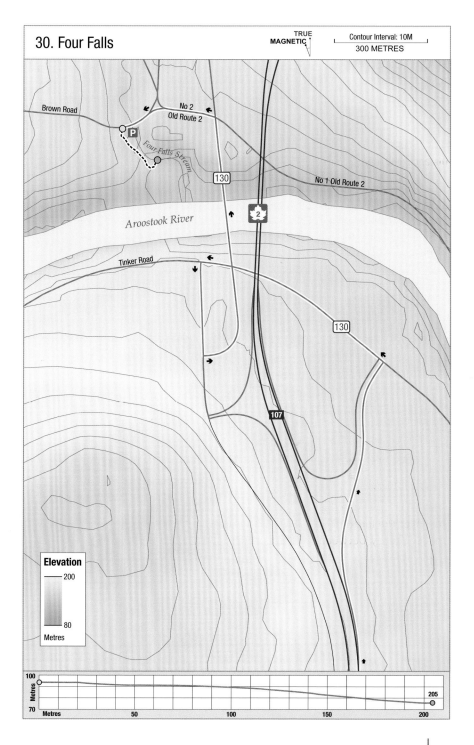

30. Four Falls

TRUE
MAGNETIC

Contour Interval: 10M

300 METRES

Brown Road

No 2
Old Route 2

P

Four Falls Stream

130

No 1 Old Route 2

2

Aroostook River

Tinker Road

130

107

Elevation

200

80

Metres

100
Metres

70
Metres

50

100

150

200

205

30. Four Falls

31. Craig Falls

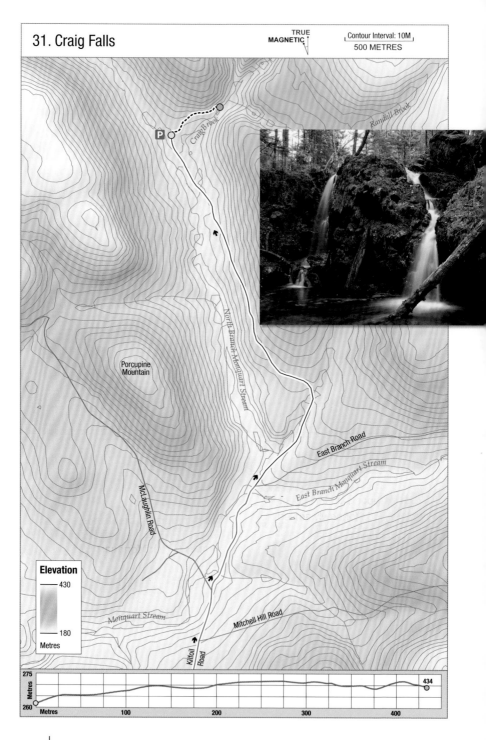

Randhill Brook

Craig Brook

Porcupine
Mountain

North Branch Monquart Stream

East Branch Road

East Branch Monquart Stream

McLaughlin Road

Elevation

430

180

Metres

Monquart Stream

Mitchell Hill Road

Kilfoil Road

275
Metres
260

434

Metres | 100 | 200 | 300 | 400

31. Craig Falls

Type: Drop
Height: 6 m
Best season(s): Summer, fall
Access: Trail
Source: Craig Brook
Distance (one way): 434 m
Difficulty: Easy

Rating: 4
Hiking time: 20 minutes
Land ownership: Private
Map: NTS 021J12 Perth-Andover
Nearby waterfall(s): Four Falls
Cellphone coverage: N

Finding the trailhead: Drive north on Route 105 through the village of Bath and, just before the bridge over the Monquart Stream, take the exit on the right for Route 565. This road leads up into the rolling hills of potato country. After Johnville, drive roughly 11 km to Murphy Corner, coordinates 46°35'07.2" N, 67°30'58.3" W. Take Kilfoil Road on the left at 46°37'32.1" N, 67°29'50.8" W and drive to the trailhead. There are a few Y junctions on the way, and the last section of this road can be rough, especially in spring.

Trailhead: 46°38'33.7" N, 67°30'40.8" W   **Waterfall:** 46°38'40.1" N, 67°30'24.9" W

The hike: This is a relaxing hike along a road through a canopy of old-growth hardwood and is exceptionally pleasing when autumn colours abound. Follow the gentle upward sweep of the ridge as it leads into the rolling hills that divide the Miramichi River and Wolastoq/Saint John River watersheds. Tucked away in the vales of these wooded hills are numerous brooks and streams, including Craig Brook and the picturesque Craig Falls. The uniqueness of the location is that there are two waterfalls; the second, tucked away behind a rock outcrop, requires a brook crossing.

Johnville was named for a Roman Catholic bishop of Saint John, John Sweeny, who acquired land in upper Carleton County in the 1860s for newly arrived Irish settlers. The region was a remote hinterland where the rolling hills were carpeted with dense, mixed forest, and the rocky soil made for poor farming. The area's Irish settlements — such as Johnville, Murphy Corner, and Kilfoil — exemplify the grit and determination of these immigrants to New Brunswick.

Bonus fall(s): Monquart Falls is located at 46°39'01.7" N, 67°31'29.7" W and can be reached by driving back down from the trailhead and up the first road on the right to the coordinates.

32. Briggs Millpond Falls

Type: Cascade
Height: 2 m
Best season(s): Spring, fall
Access: Road
Source: Little Shikatehawk Stream
Distance (one way): 25 m
Difficulty: Easy

Rating: 3
Hiking time: 5 minutes
Land ownership: Crown
Map: NTS 021J05 Florenceville
Nearby waterfall(s): Craig Falls
Cellphone coverage: Y

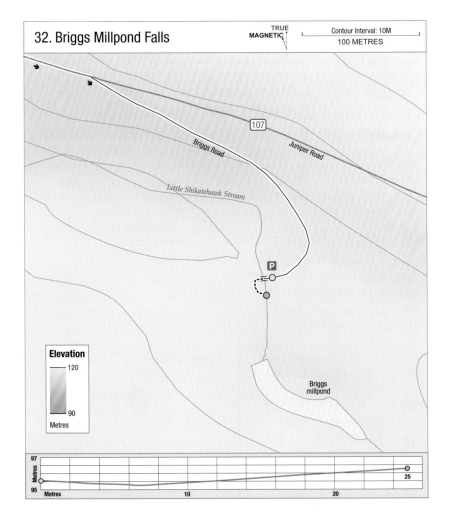

Finding the trailhead: Head to the town of Florenceville-Bristol in Carleton County. From Florenceville proper, drive north along Route 105 to Bristol. In Bristol, take Route 107 on the right and drive toward Juniper. Roughly 1.4 km up the road, turn right onto Briggs Road. Drive slowly down the road to the small bridge spanning the Little Shikatehawk Stream and park on the side of the road before the bridge.

Trailhead: 46°28'0.3" N, 67°33'38.3" W   **Waterfall:** 46°28'02.6" N, 67°33'38.2" W

The hike: Although Briggs Road is municipal, the adjacent properties are private and must be respected. To see the falls, walk across the bridge and immediately head upstream about 30 m to a rock ledge with a great view of the waterfall, with the Briggs millpond in the background. Little Shikatehawk Stream was used to power the Giberson family sawmill in the 1860s, creating the millpond. Family members told me that the mill was in operation when Canada became a unified country in 1867. The mill was later owned and operated by William Briggs, who manufactured window sashes and other building fixtures. The location is certainly steeped in Carleton County history.

33. Jennings Falls

TRUE
MAGNETIC

Contour Interval: 10M
1 KILOMETRE

Elevation

190

50

Metres

105

Jennings Road

Ackers Creek

Ackers Creek
Bridge

Sentier NB Trail

P

150

Metres

107

100

Metres 10 20 30 40 50 60 70 80 90 100

33. Jennings Falls

Type: Tiered
Height: 8 m
Best season(s): Spring, summer, fall
Access: Trail
Source: Ackers Creek
Distance (one way): 107 m
Difficulty: Easy to moderate

Rating: 4
Hiking time: 10 minutes
Land ownership: Private
Map: NTS 021J03 Millville
Nearby waterfall(s): Gibson Creek Falls
Cellphone coverage: Y

Finding the trailhead: From Woodstock, drive across the Wolastoq/Saint John River to Grafton and turn left onto Route 105. Drive approximately 5 km north toward Hartland until reaching the Ackers Creek Bridge. Immediately after the bridge, turn right onto Jennings Road, named for a family of Irish immigrants that homesteaded along the creek. Drive up the road roughly 2.5 km to the trailhead.

Trailhead: 46°13'12.4" N, 67°28'16.5" W **Waterfall:** 46°13'14.1" N, 67°28'13.3" W

The hike: The trailhead is in a small clearing under a large pine tree. From the pine, follow the narrow path over and down a steep incline into the ravine. A good level of physical fitness is required to access Jennings Falls. The ridges on either side rise abruptly from the creek, keeping the area rich with moisture and slippery and making the hike strenuous. The site is beautiful and is especially stunning in autumn, a "must see" for waterfall enthusiasts. The creek has cut a deep gulley through the valley, except here at an outcrop of bedrock where the falls are. The timeless energy of this narrow creek etched a notch in the rock at the top of the upper falls and then found a second fissure, where it cut a second notch for the stream to drop over the lower falls and into a large pool, before continuing southwesterly to the Wolastoq/Saint John River.

34. Millseat Falls

TRUE
MAGNETIC

Contour Interval: 10M
2 KILOMETRES

power line
585
West Branch Nackawic Stream
Nortondale

Elevation
200
120
Metres

140
Metres
134
Metres   1   2   3   4   5   6   7   8   9
9.1

34. Millseat Falls

Type: Tiered
Height: 5 m
Best season(s): Spring, summer, fall
Access: Roadside
Source: West Branch Nackawic Stream
Distance (one way): 9.1 m
Difficulty: Easy

Rating: 2
Hiking time: 1 minute
Land ownership: Crown
Map: NTS 021J03 Millville
Nearby waterfall(s): Gibson Creek Falls
Cellphone coverage: Y

Finding the trailhead: From the Grafton Bridge in Woodstock, head east on Route 585 to Nortondale. Drive roughly 22 km and, just before crossing the West Branch Nackawic Stream, park alongside the road at the trailhead. Be careful when parking and crossing the road to the trailhead as this is a relatively busy highway.

Trailhead: 46°06'55.3" N, 67°18'51.6" W **Waterfall:** 46°06'55.6" N, 67°18'51.8" W

The hike: This waterfall has no need for a trail. Located near the road, the river has sculpted a rock face that provides a good view of the waterfall. Caution must be exercised, as the drop from the treeline to the stream is 5 m. The West Branch Nackawic Stream cascades over a bedrock outcrop and is divided into three separate channels that reconnect in a pool near the rock face. This appealing waterfall is a delight to photograph, especially in autumn with a background of softwood and a sprinkling of maple and birch to highlight the scene. A roadside treasure, it is obscured from view by the thick curtain of spruce and cedar that dominates the edges of the stream. Many people commuting to Woodstock for work drive by Millseat Falls on a daily basis without noticing it.

35. Gibson Creek Falls

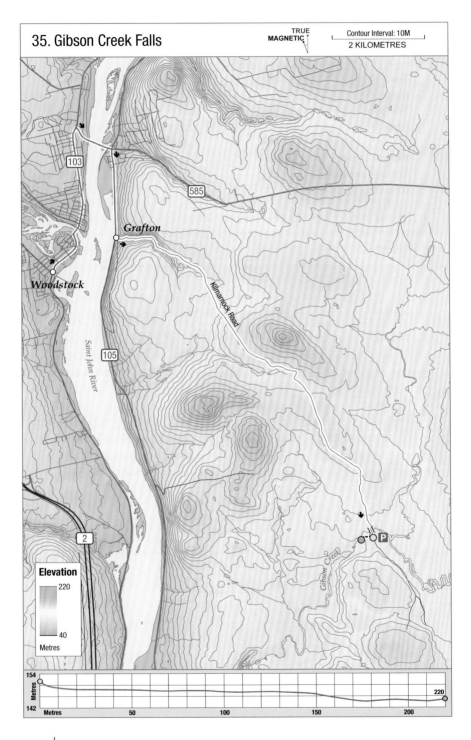

TRUE
MAGNETIC

Contour Interval: 10M

2 KILOMETRES

103

585

Grafton

Kilmarnock Road

Woodstock

Saint John River

105

2

Elevation

220

40

Metres

Gibson Creek

P

154
Metres
142

Metres

50

100

150

200

220

35. Gibson Creek Falls

Type: Tiered
Height: 10 m
Best season(s): Spring, summer, fall
Access: Trail
Source: Gibson Creek
Distance (one way): 220 m
Difficulty: Easy

Rating: 3
Hiking time: 10 minutes
Land ownership: Crown
Map: NTS 021J03 Millville
Nearby waterfall(s): Jennings Falls, Hays Falls
Cellphone coverage: Y

Finding the trailhead: From the town of Woodstock, cross the Wolastoq/Saint John River to Grafton. At the intersection with Route 105, turn right and drive downriver 2 km to the turnoff for Kilmarnock Road on the left. This access road winds upward into the hills away from the valley. Follow the gravel road a distance of 11.5 km until crossing over the bridge that spans Gibson Creek. The trailhead to the waterfall is on the right immediately after the bridge.

Trailhead: 46°05'30.5" N, 67°29'30.5" W **Waterfall:** 46°05'29.7" N, 67°29'39.5" W

The hike: Follow the marked trail from the trailhead to the apex of Gibson Creek Falls. It is located at a transition point where the uplands that overlook the

Wolastoq/Saint John River valley moderate into rolling hills that sweep down to the river. The gentle character of the Kilmarnock Deadwater changes abruptly at the escarpment, where the creek drops through a notch in the bedrock to form this double-tiered waterfall that crashes into a generous basin.

The waterfall is named after William Gibson, who emigrated to Canada from Kilmarnock, Scotland, and helped establish a farming settlement in the area in 1843. The deep, dark bowl at the base of the falls makes this is a very popular place for swimming and fishing. There is a rock face adjacent to the falls that illustrates the enormous pressure these rock formations have undergone in the geological past. The stratum is twisted first up and then straight down, forming the letter *S* on its side. Large pine trees surround the falls, which have several excellent vantage points from which to photograph.

36. Hays Falls

Type: Fan
Height: 24 m
Best season(s): Year-round
Access: Trail
Source: Hays Brook
Distance (one way): 1.5 km
Difficulty: Easy to moderate

Rating: 5
Hiking time: 1 hour
Land ownership: Crown
Map: NTS 021J04 Woodstock
Nearby waterfall(s): Gibson Creek Falls
Cellphone coverage: Y

Finding the trailhead: Driving north on Route 2 (TCH) from Fredericton, take exit 212 at Meductic. At the stop sign, turn right and drive down the hill on Route 165. At the intersection, turn left and continue west upriver on Route 165 for an additional 7 km to a lookout on the left with a large sign indicating the Maliseet Trail. There is adequate parking available regardless of the season since the trailhead is maintained throughout the winter.

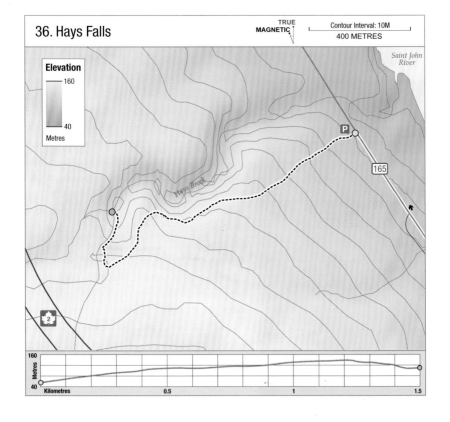

Trailhead: 46°01'45.3" N, 67°32'35.3" W
Waterfall: 46°01'35.0" N, 67°33'18.9" W

The hike: The trailhead for this 1.5 km hike begins at the welcome sign. Follow the bear paw signage as the trail gently ascends through a mixed forest and eventually leads through a grove of old-growth softwoods. After the crest of the hill, the trail rises and falls until reaching a sign that indicates a path on the left up to the top of the falls, and one on the right down into the basin. The trail down into the ravine can be slippery, even during the driest months.

Hays Falls is Carleton County's most impressive waterfall and one of the top ten in New Brunswick. Without a doubt, it is one of the most widely known and visited falls in our province. This fan falls attracts visitors year-round, offering an area to rest and enjoy the natural surroundings in every season. In winter, the face is frequently utilized by ice-climbing enthusiasts from nearby clubs. The well-maintained trail makes it family friendly, but it can become somewhat muddy after a heavy rain.

37. Eel River Falls

TRUE
MAGNETIC

Contour Interval: 10M
500 METRES

power line

Eel River

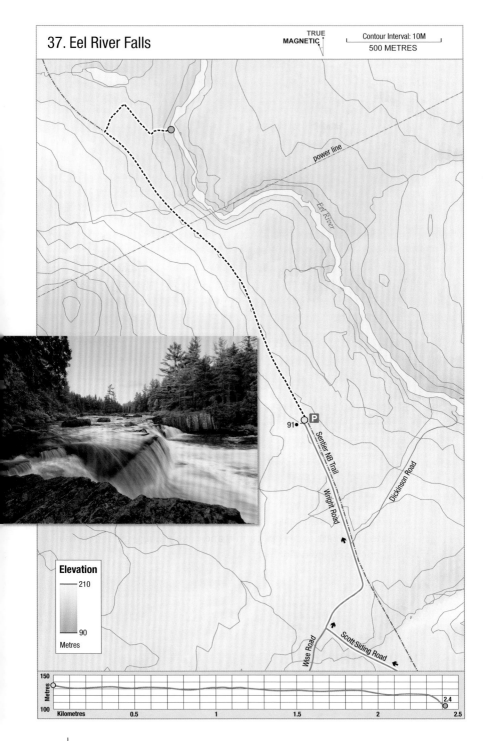

91• ○ P

Sentier NB Trail

Wright Road

Dickinson Road

Elevation
— 210

— 90
Metres

Wise Road

Scott Siding Road

150
Metres
100
Kilometres   0.5   1   1.5   2   2.5

2.4

37. Eel River Falls

Type: Drop
Height: 2.5 m
Best season(s): Summer, fall
Access: Trail
Source: Eel River
Distance (one way): 2.4 km
Difficulty: Easy

Rating: 3
Hiking time: 1 hour
Land ownership: Crown
Map: NTS 021G14 Canterbury
Nearby waterfall(s): Hays Falls, Sullivan Creek Falls
Cellphone coverage: Y

Finding the trailhead: Drive on Route 122 to the village of Canterbury. On Main Street (Route 122) look for Mill Street. Drive out Mill Street 2.3 km to the end. Turn left and drive 300 m to Scott Siding Road on the right. Drive out the road 6.2 km until it ends at a T junction and turn right onto Wise Road. Head out this road and, where it becomes Wright Road, continue on that road to 91 Wright Road, a distance of 1.2 km. Opposite that house is an entrance to the old railbed, which is now part of the Sentier NB Trail system. Rarely used by hikers, it has become an ATV trail. There is sufficient area to park.

Trailhead: 45°56'11.4" N, 67°33'27.2" W   **Waterfall:** 45°57'01.1" N, 67°34'01.2" W

The hike: From the parking area trailhead, begin hiking or mountain biking roughly 2 km to a woods road on the right. Walk roughly 180 m down to the first road on the right. Walk out on this road, and there is a narrow trail on the left within 200 m that leads to the waterfall. The crash of the waterfall can be heard all the way from the trailhead. Caution is required near the falls because the trail twists and turns around large rock outcrops.

Eel River Falls is a series of three-tiered cascades over sheer ledges, spanning the majestic Eel River. Several large boulders stretch out from the bank into the channel, perfect for viewing this beautiful waterfall. The river drains a large area to the northwest comprised of several large wetlands and lakes, and for the most part, it sweeps calmly and gently along, guided by the low hills that dominate the region.

38. Sullivan Creek Falls

Type: Cascade
Height: 20 m
Best season(s): Spring, fall
Access: Bushwhack
Source: Sullivan Creek
Distance (one way): 1.2 km
Difficulty: Moderate

Rating: 5
Hiking time: 1 hour
Land ownership: Crown
Map: NTS 021G14 Canterbury
Nearby waterfall(s): Hays Falls
Cellphone coverage: N

Finding the trailhead: From Nackawic, drive north toward Meductic on Route 2 (TCH), watching for kilometre marker 218. Roughly 400 m past the marker, there is a deer gate on the righthand side of the highway at the trailhead.

Trailhead: 45°56'59.1" N, 67°25'01.3" W **Waterfall:** 45°57'15.0" N, 67°24'33.9" W

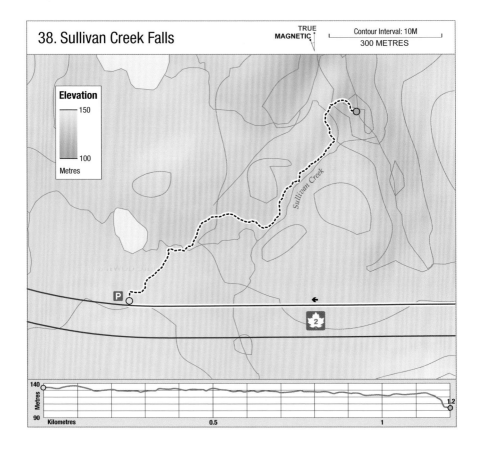

The hike: There is no defined hiking trail to the waterfall. Go through the deer gate and head east along the fence toward a small clearing to the left of the fence. Cross the clearing to an opening in the forest canopy where, with help from a friend, I cut branches and tied tape indicating the route. Follow the orange marking tape to a small brook — there are three brooks in the vicinity. The trail requires a jump across a brook at a location just above a small waterfall. Follow the marking tape and the contour of the land with the creek on the right to the edge of the ravine, and follow the route down and around the waterfall to the base. At the base, the creek rushes over and around large angular boulders. Note that this hike can be wet underfoot, especially in the spring.

The creek is gentle until it begins to hasten and carve through bedrock on its journey to the Wolastoq/Saint John River. There are several drops and slides at the top of the falls before it plunges into the ravine, making the waterfall appear much higher than expected. I have driven past this location numerous times, speculating whether the valley contained a waterfall. After asking around, a friend told me there was one, but he could not remember how high it was. In the spring of 2020, we went there and were both surprised by the height of the waterfall.

39. Big Falls (Shogomoc)

Type: Cascade
Height: 5 m
Best season(s): Spring, summer, fall
Access: Trail, bushwhack
Source: Shogomoc Stream
Distance (one way): 1.1 km
Difficulty: Moderate

Rating: 5
Hiking time: 1 hour
Land ownership: Crown
Map: NTS 021G14 Canterbury
Nearby waterfall(s): Hays Falls
Cellphone coverage: Y

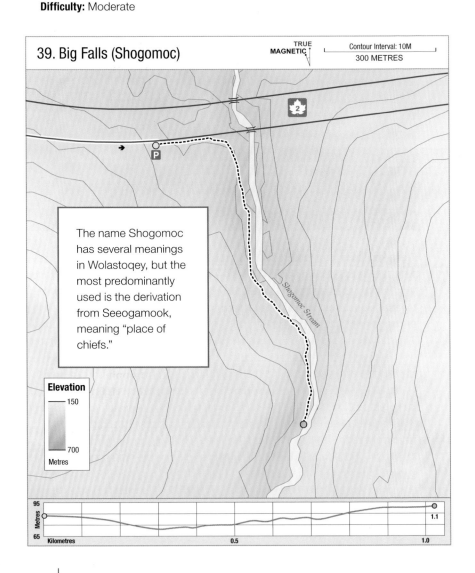

39. Big Falls (Shogomoc)

TRUE MAGNETIC

Contour Interval: 10M
300 METRES

The name Shogomoc has several meanings in Wolastoqey, but the most predominantly used is the derivation from Seeogamook, meaning "place of chiefs."

Shogomoc Stream

Elevation
150
700
Metres

Finding the trailhead: Drive south from Woodstock on Route 2 (TCH) to 45°56'54.6" N, 67°19'32.5" W and park before the bridge spanning the Shogomoc Stream. For safety, pull off the highway and park behind the guardrail.

Trailhead: 45°56'54.6" N, 67°19'32.5" W   **Waterfall:** 45°56'30.5" N, 67°19'14.2" W

The hike: There is no defined trail, so walk toward the stream. Just before it, push through the woods on the edge of the clearing and head upstream. The forest has naturally thinned, and there is a partial trail, so hiking is very easy. The demeanor of the stream from Shogomoc Lake is rather gentle for the most part as it collects waters from wetlands. This serene character drastically changes roughly 2 km up from the confluence with the Wolastoq/Saint John River, where the stream knifes through the mountainside, dropping quickly. In a section of 300 m, the stream has four beautiful waterfalls of which Shogomoc Falls and Big Falls are predominant.

This stream is a magical "must-see" for people who enjoy a relaxing walk in the woods. There are numerous places along the stream to sit and enjoy the wild natural surroundings. The coordinates above are for Big Falls, the third of the four waterfalls, which tumbles over a sheer ledge spanning the stream and is slightly higher than its brethren. There are several large granite outcrops on which to sit and contemplate life, and enjoy the beautiful soothing sound of the water as it splashes over and around the large boulders. The maple, beech, and birch overstorey completes a picturesque scene.

40. Coac Stream Falls

Type: Tiered
Height: 21 m
Best season(s): Spring, fall
Access: Trail
Source: Coac Lake
Distance (one way): 2.2 km
Difficulty: Easy to moderate

Rating: 5
Hiking time: 1 hour 20 minutes
Land ownership: Private
Map: NTS 021G14 Canterbury
Nearby waterfall(s): Howland Falls
Cellphone coverage: Y

Finding the trailhead: At the junction of Route 605 and Route 105 in the town of Nackawic, drive south on Route 105 along the Wolastoq/Saint John River for approximately 7 km to coordinates 45°58'47.8" N, 67°09'26.3" W. Drive 550 m up the old woods road on the left, formerly known as Lower Caverhill Road, and park. The trailhead is located opposite the parking area.

Trailhead: 45°59'03.7" N, 67°09'12.9" W   **Waterfall:** 46°00'02.8" N, 67°09'02.4" W

The hike: The pleasant hike up to the waterfall is mostly through old-growth forest, except for a short section of clearcut. From the parking area, follow the road opposite for 400 m to the top of the ridge. You will see a clearcut on your left, a road straight ahead, and the road on the right that you take. Follow the ridgeline as it curves gently to the left until a Y in the road. Take the road on the right for roughly 1.2 km until reaching an ATV trail on the left and the steep trail leading down to the base of the falls.

Coac is one of those waterfalls where its character carries you away as you descend into the ravine. At 21 m, it is among the higher waterfalls in this region and is easily one of the most picturesque in the province. The name is Wolastoqey for "pine tree in the distance," and there are numerous large pine trees found along the ridges and escarpments. This waterfall is on private property, so please respect ownership and carry out everything you carry in.

40. Coac Stream Falls

TRUE
MAGNETIC

Contour Interval: 10M
500 METRES

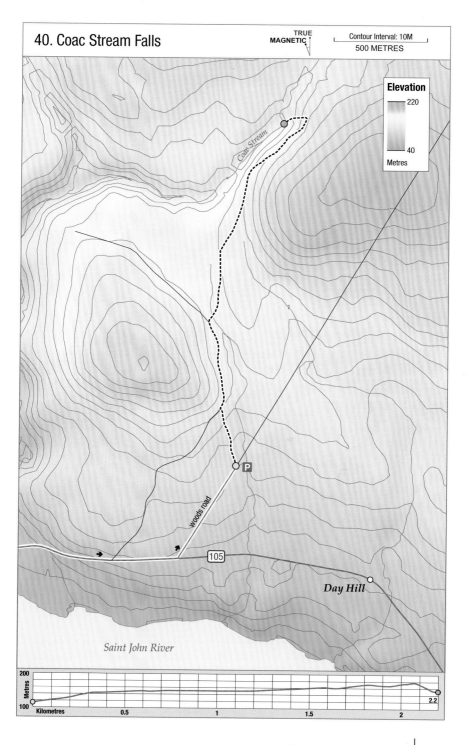

Elevation
220

40
Metres

Coac Stream

P

woods road

105

Day Hill

Saint John River

40. Coac Stream Falls

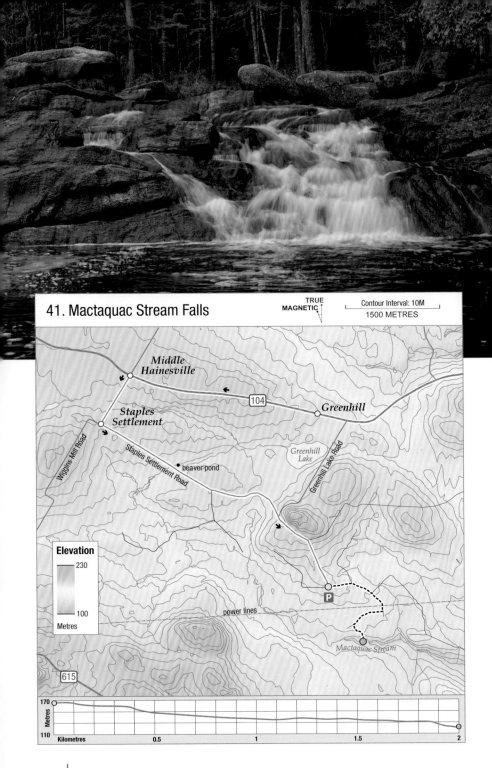

41. Mactaquac Stream Falls

TRUE
MAGNETIC

Contour Interval: 10M
1500 METRES

Middle
Hainesville

Staples
Settlement

104

Greenhill

Wiggins Mill Road

Staples Settlement Road

• beaver pond

Greenhill
Lake

Greenhill Lake Road

Elevation

230

100

Metres

power lines

P

Mactaquac Stream

615

170

110

Metres

Kilometres   0.5   1   1.5   2

41. Mactaquac Stream Falls

Type: Cascade
Height: 8 m
Best season(s): Summer, fall
Access: Trail
Source: Mactaquac Stream
Distance (one way): 2 km
Difficulty: Easy

Rating: 3
Hiking time: 1 hour
Land ownership: Private
Map: NTS 021J02 Burtts Corner
Nearby waterfall(s): Howland Falls
Cellphone coverage: Y

Finding the trailhead: Drive Route 104 through Burtts Corner and Zealand toward Crabbe Mountain. At Wiggins Mill Road turn left, and drive about 900 m. Turn left again and drive out on Staples Settlement Road. There is a beaver pond along the way that may cover the road, depending on water levels. At approximately 2 km, stay left and, after 4 km, turn right at 46°02'57.6" N, 67°02'10.9 W and drive downhill through a clearcut to a T junction. It is possible to drive further, but the road gets rough, so I recommend parking here.

Trailhead: 46°02'33.7" N, 67°01'54.5" W **Waterfall:** 46°02'06.2" N, 67°01'29.7" W

The hike: Begin walking along the road in an easterly direction as it makes a swing to the south and eventually emerges from the trees at a set of power-lines. Just beyond, follow a narrow logging road on the right that heads west to the trailhead, a distance of roughly 600 m. Note that the original trail from Green Hill Camp has changed due to the clearcut but is still marked, following a twisting and turning route through a mature forest of pine and assorted hardwoods. Near the falls, the trail is covered in a bed of pine needles with large boulders, an excellent place to sit and enjoy nature at its finest. It is also the preferred swimming area for kids attending the nearby Green Hill Camp. The waterfall nestles at the base of Green Hill, spanning the entire stream, and forms a large pool before continuing eastward. During the spring freshet, the roar of the falls carries down the broad valley and across the Mactaquac headpond.

42. Howland Falls

Type: Tiered
Height: 11 m
Best season(s): Year-round
Access: Trail
Source: Sinnots Brook
Distance (one way): 111 m
Difficulty: Easy

Rating: 3
Hiking time: 4 minutes
Land ownership: Private
Map: NTS 021G14 Canterbury
Nearby waterfall(s): Mactaquac
Stream Falls, Coac Stream Falls
Cellphone coverage: Y

Finding the trailhead: From the main entrance to Mactaquac Provincial Park, drive Route 105 for roughly 19.5 km along the Mactaquac headpond. Turn right onto Scotch Lake Road and drive up the gravel road to the cement bridge, a distance of 840 m. The trailhead and parking area are located just before the bridge. This can be a busy place at times since it is a well-known waterfall in the greater Fredericton region.

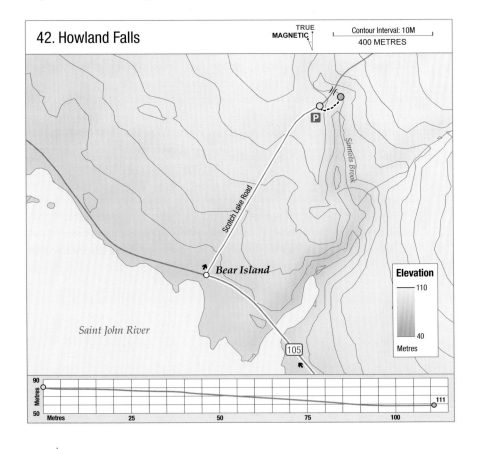

Trailhead: 45°55'40.2" N, 67°01'12.9" W **Waterfall:** 45°55'41.5" N, 67°01'09.4" W

The hike: The path down to the falls is just before the bridge on your right. The trail can be slippery near the bottom before leveling off at the base of the falls, where there is an excellent viewing area. The picturesque stream cascades down from the hills flanking the Wolastoq/Saint John River. At approximately 11 m, Howland Falls is not extremely high, but it has its own distinctive character. Situated in an old stand of pine, the ravine is refreshingly cool on a hot summer day. Large boulders and trees, ripped from the stream's edge, are strewn about the pool at its base.

Nothing remains of the old Howland gristmill that stood alongside the waterfalls at the turn of the last century. The property still belongs to the Howland family, who do not mind visitors as long as the area is kept clean. Enjoy the beautiful scenery of the Mactaquac headpond and the Bear Island area on the drive to Howland Falls, as Route 105 meanders through farmland and cottage country. In autumn, the hardwood ridges come alive in a cornucopia of colours.

43. Lower Joslin Creek Falls

TRUE
MAGNETIC

Contour Interval: 10M
50 METRES

Elevation

100

60

Metres

deer
gate

Joslin Creek

P

2

88
Metres
80

71

Metres   10   20   30   40   50   60   70

43. Lower Joslin Creek Falls

Type: Drop
Height: 6 m
Best season(s): Year-round
Access: Trail
Source: Joslin Creek
Distance (one way): 71 m
Difficulty: Easy to moderate

Rating: 4
Hiking time: 15 minutes
Land ownership: Crown
Map: NTS 021G14 Canterbury
Nearby waterfall(s): Split Rock Falls, Upper Joslin Creek Falls
Cellphone coverage: Y

Finding the trailhead: Lower Joslin Creek Falls is located alongside Route 2 (TCH) west of Fredericton, approximately 5 km past the turnoff to the Kings Landing historic village. The falls can be reached by parking beside the highway at the 250 km marker and hiking through the deer gate, which is the trailhead and the access to the trail.

Trailhead: 45°53'09.9" N, 67°01'32.1" W   **Waterfall:** 45°53'10.9" N, 67°01'30.2" W

The hike: A stone's throw away from the northbound lanes of Route 2 (TCH) is one of the finer roadside waterfalls in New Brunswick. The creek drops vertically a distance of 6 m into a ravine strewn with sizeable boulders. Even though the waterfall is very close to the highway, the sound of the water crashing into the large boulders and the surrounding cliffs provide a barrier, making it easy to forget the noisy traffic.

The coordinates above are to the top of the waterfall and, despite the short distance, watch your footing. The path twists over and around boulders, and near the top of the falls, there is a vertical drop-off. There are a few different trails down into the ravine, leading to locations from which to capture a photo keepsake. The path on the right side of the ravine requires climbing down large moss-covered boulders. The effort is rewarded upon reaching an excellent vantage point directly in front of the falls.

Bonus fall(s): Upper Joslin Creek Falls is located further up the brook on the opposite side of Route 2 at 45°53'06.0" N, 67°01'34.9" W

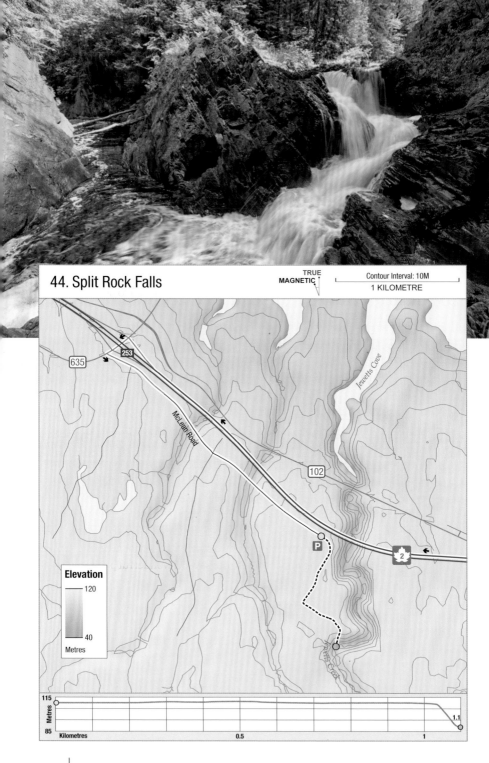

44. Split Rock Falls

TRUE
MAGNETIC

Contour Interval: 10M
1 KILOMETRE

635
253
McLean Road
Jewetts Cove
102
2
Fretts Croix

Elevation
120

40
Metres

115
Metres
85
Kilometres
0.5
1
1.1

44. Split Rock Falls

Type: Cascade
Height: 6 m
Best season(s): Spring, summer, fall
Access: Trail
Source: Jewetts Creek
Distance (one way): 1.1 km
Difficulty: Moderate

Rating: 4
Hiking time: 30 minutes
Land ownership: Private
Map: NTS 021G15 Fredericton
Nearby waterfall(s): Lower Joslin Creek Falls
Cellphone coverage: Y

Finding the trailhead: Drive north on Route 2 (TCH) and take exit 253 toward the Kings Landing historic village. At the intersection, turn left and drive approximately 200 m on Route 635. Turn left onto McLean Road and drive roughly 2.2 km to the parking area and trailhead. The brush along the logging road beyond is beginning to grow in, so use this parking area to avoid vehicle scratches.

Trailhead: 45°51'36.7" N, 66°57'46.2" W **Waterfall:** 45°51'09.6" N, 66°57'41.0" W

The hike: From the trailhead, walk along the logging road roughly 620 m to a small turning area on the left. At this location, there is a trail leading into the old clearcut. Follow this trail to the top of the ravine and then down to a narrow ridge overlooking the waterfall. From this location, the view is straight down to the falls. It is particularly dramatic during the spring freshet or after a few days of heavy rain.

Split Rock was given its name by loggers around 1900 when the original fall was blasted to dislodge jammed timber during the spring lumber drive. The blast left a unique turn where the stream gushes down through a split in the rock, smashing against a solid granite wall at the base. From here, it is forced into a sharp right turn and then another granite outcrop forces a sharp left bend. Further downstream, there are two smaller falls that give this section of the stream a stunning impact. There are several wonderful pools and small rapids below the ravine.

After the publication of my first book on waterfalls, I was contacted by a sweet elderly lady with a wonderful story of romance. I was informed that, about the turn of the last century, her grandfather proposed to her grandmother at this waterfall.

45. Pete Brook Falls

TRUE
MAGNETIC

Contour Interval: 10M

500 METRES

Pete Brook

access road

Duplisea Road

South Branch Oromocto River

Elevation
— 140

— 10

Metres

Smythe
Covered
Bridge

West Mill Settlement Road

Mill Settlement Road

98

Metres

83

822

Metres 100 200 300 400 500 600 700 800

45. Pete Brook Falls

Type: Drop
Height: 5 m
Best season(s): Spring, fall
Access: Trail, river walk
Source: Pete Brook
Distance (one way): 822 m
Difficulty: Easy to moderate

Rating: 2
Hiking time: 25 minutes
Land ownership: Private
Map: NTS 021G10 Fredericton Junction
Nearby waterfall(s): Carrow Brook Falls, Raggedy Ass Falls
Cellphone coverage: Y

Finding the trailhead: Drive south on Route 101 to the rural community of Hoyt. Look for Mill Settlement Road on the right. Drive approximately 2.4 km on it and turn right onto West Mill Settlement Road. Drive down the hill and across the covered bridge to the junction with Duplisea Road. Turn right onto Duplisea Road and drive 300 m to the access road on the left. If the access road is washed out, park here and walk up — or try to drive — to the trailhead.

Trailhead: 45°34'59.3" N, 66°35'16.9" W **Waterfall:** 45°34'54.0□ N, 66°35'44.2□ W

The hike: From the woods road, it is a gentle twenty-minute ascent to the falls along a beautiful multiuse trail. Roughly 600 m into the trail, it turns to the left. The walking bridge that crossed the brook is washed out, creating a brook crossing. The trail leads to the top of the falls so, once across, follow the west side of the brook down the trail to the bottom to enjoy a full view of the falls. There is a rope to help with the descent into the ravine. Pete Brook Falls is nestled in a beautiful woodland setting. This is a very enjoyable hike, especially in autumn.

I have a framed collage of two four-leaf clovers on my desk. As I write about this waterfall, I am reminded of my dear friend Elmo MacDonald of Fredericton Junction, who worked diligently with the Oromocto River Watershed. The collage, a gift from Elmo, is a symbol of the good fortune that, through our common interest in waterfalls, we became good friends. Elmo was very proud of the trails he made to several waterfalls scattered along the eastern ridges of the Juvenile Hills, especially this one at Pete Brook Falls.

46. Carrow Brook Falls

TRUE
MAGNETIC

Contour Interval: 10M
500 METRES

46. Carrow Brook Falls

Type: Fan
Height: 5 m
Best season(s): Spring, fall
Access: Trail
Source: Carrow Brook
Distance (one way): 287 m
Difficulty: Easy to moderate

Rating: 2
Hiking time: 20 minutes
Land ownership: Private
Map: NTS 021G10 Fredericton Junction
Nearby waterfall(s): Sand Brook Falls, Raggedy Ass Falls
Cellphone coverage: Y

Finding the trailhead: Drive south on Route 101 through the community of Hoyt. Look for the Mill Settlement Road on the right. Drive out the road approximately 2.4 km and turn right onto the West Mill Settlement Road. Drive down the hill and cross the Smyth Covered Bridge to the junction with Duplisea Road. Stay left and drive about 2 km until you see the access road on the left at 45°34'08.7" N, 66°36'14.0" W. Turn and drive roughly 600 m to a parking area on the left. This is the trailhead.

Trailhead: 45°33'50.1" N, 66°36'19.8" W   **Waterfall:** 45°33'47.5" N, 66°36'11.7" W

The hike: Walk down the road, turn left just beyond Carrow Brook, and follow the trail downstream, making sure to stay close to the brook until you eventually come to a small wooden bridge. The trail is wet prior to the short descent to the base of the falls, especially in spring and late autumn. Carrow is a small brook that fades away during summer, and in an overly warm autumn, the waterfall tapers to a scant dribble. It is yet another diminutive brook, tumbling down the eastern flank of the Juvenile Hills to form the Oromocto River watershed.

The Oromocto River Watershed Association urges visitors to stay on the designated path as it is important not to walk or climb on the moss-covered falls. This is an environmentally sensitive area, wholly covered with a thick blanket of moss, and rare plants are found along the brook.

47. Scribner Brook Falls

Type: Drop
Height: 1.5 m
Best season(s): Spring, fall
Access: Trail
Source: Scribner Brook
Distance (one way): 42 m
Difficulty: Easy

Rating: 2
Hiking time: 5 minutes
Land ownership: Private
Map: NTS 021G10 Fredericton Junction
Nearby waterfall(s): Carrow Brook Falls, Raggedy Ass Falls
Cellphone coverage: Y

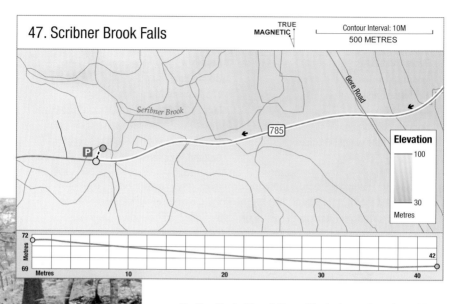

47. Scribner Brook Falls

TRUE
MAGNETIC

Contour Interval: 10M
500 METRES

Scribner Brook

785

Elevation
— 100

— 30
Metres

72
Metres
69

42

Metres   10   20   30   40

Finding the trailhead: From Fredericton Junction, drive Route 101 on the lookout for Route 785 on the right, before the community of Hoyt. Drive roughly 170 m on Route 785, turn right, and continue straight on Route 785 into the Juvenile Hills approximately 2 km to the trailhead, located along the roadside. There is sufficient space to park safely.

Trailhead: 45°37'10.1" N, 66°36'27.8" W
Waterfall: 45°37'11.3□ N, 66°36'26.9□ W

The hike: A mere 50 m from Route 785, Scribner Brook Falls is one of New Brunswick's roadside waterfalls that is perfect for families with small children or folks with mobility issues to visit. The path is relatively flat and free of debris. When there is sufficient water, this small waterfall in the Juvenile Hills perks up and provides a beautiful show for those who take a few minutes to stop and explore. For further exploration, visitors can mosey down along the brook to a good location to photograph the waterfall. The site is maintained by the Oromocto River Watershed Association.

48. Raggedy Ass Falls

Type: Tiered
Height: Various
Best season(s): Spring, fall
Access: Trail
Source: Nutter Brook
Distance (one way): 658 m
Difficulty: Easy

Rating: 4
Hiking time: 20 minutes
Land ownership: Private
Map: NTS 021G07 McDougall Lake
Nearby waterfall(s): Sand Brook Falls, Carrow Brook Falls
Cellphone coverage: Y

Finding the trailhead: From Fredericton Junction, drive toward Hoyt on Route 101 on the lookout for Route 785 on the right. Drive roughly 170 m on Route 785 and turn right again to continue on 785 — straight becomes Duplisea Road. Drive roughly 20 km to the access road, located on the left at 45°30'38.4" N, 66°45'14.4" W. This is the western terminus of Sand Brook Road. Head east on Sand Brook Road, taking the left turn at 45°30'27.7" N, 66°43'11.0" W. Continue roughly 8.3 km and park next to the logging road on the right.

Trailhead: 45°29'51.0" N, 66°37'22.5" W
Waterfall: 45°29'57.4" N, 66°36'59.4" W

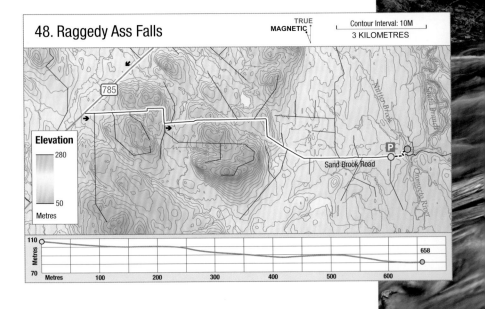

48. Raggedy Ass Falls

TRUE
MAGNETIC

Contour Interval: 10M
3 KILOMETRES

Elevation
280
50
Metres

110
Metres
70

Metres 100 200 300 400 500 600

658

The hike: From the parking location, walk down Sand Brook Road roughly 420 m and turn left onto the hiking trail. It is a short hike to this beautiful complex of waterfalls and its excellent swimming holes. Large rocks surrounding the area provide a wonderful venue to sit and enjoy this splendid wilderness. Nutter Brook flows in a southeasterly direction, dropping through a series of twisting rock outcrops before converging with the South Branch Oromocto River.

Raggedy Ass is an appropriate unofficial name for the falls and trail. The brook bounces over and around the twisting and turning bedrock in what could be considered a ragged route. Take time to explore the series of five waterfalls that drop a total of 20 m. The falls are very striking, especially the uppermost one, which is formed as the brook slides over the rock face into a large pool.

49. Hubble Brook Falls

TRUE
MAGNETIC

Contour Interval: 10M
3 KILOMETRES

785

Elevation

280

50

Metres

Sand Brook Road

P

Miller Brook

Mill Branch

Comocto River

Hubble Brook

130
Metres
110

Metres   10   20   30   40   50

56

49. Hubble Brook Falls

Type: Tiered
Height: 5 m
Best season(s): Spring, fall
Access: Trail
Source: Hubble Brook
Distance (one way): 56 m
Difficulty: Easy

Rating: 2
Hiking time: 5 minutes
Land ownership: Private
Map: NTS 021G07 McDougall Lake
Nearby waterfall(s): Raggedy Ass Falls, Carrow Falls
Cellphone coverage: Y

Finding the trailhead: From Fredericton Junction, drive toward Hoyt on Route 101 on the lookout for Route 785 on the right. Drive roughly 170 m and turn right again to continue on Route 785 — straight becomes Duplisea Road. Drive roughly 20 km to the access road located on the left at 45°30'38.4" N, 66°45'14.4" W. This is the western terminus of Sand Brook Road. Head east on Sand Brook Road, taking the left turn at 45°30'27.7" N, 66°43'11.0" W. Continue roughly 7 km and turn right onto the logging road at 45°29'50.1" N, 66°38'07.1" W. Drive roughly 600 m to the parking area and trailhead on the left, just before the bridge over Hubble Brook.

Trailhead: 45°29'33.3" N, 66°38'18.9" W **Waterfall:** 45°29'32.9" N, 66°38'16.6" W

The hike: There are two waterfalls located within 100 m of each other. The more impressive is the lower Hubble Falls. The path leading to the falls is relatively flat, but the gorge is 6 m deep, and the banks can be slippery due to the moist spray floating up from the falls. Practice caution when climbing down to take photos from an alternative perspective below the falls. To see the upper waterfall, simply backtrack to the road and walk up along Hubble Brook.

According to the Oromocto River Watershed Association, a man named Hubble moved from Connecticut in the 1800s to set up a sawmill here. In his first winter, an unseasonable January thaw destroyed the waterwheel powering his mill. He moved back to Connecticut, but his name remains.

50. Sand Brook Falls

TRUE
MAGNETIC

Contour Interval: 10M
400 METRES

Elevation
— 220
— 150
Metres

Ogden Road

P

Sand Brook

168
Metres
160

Metres   50   100   150

199

50. **Sand Brook Falls**

Type: Drop
Height: 3 m
Best season(s): Spring, fall
Access: Trail
Source: Sand Brook
Distance (one way): 199 m
Difficulty: Easy

Rating: 3
Hiking time: 20 minutes
Land ownership: Private
Map: NTS 021G08 Saint John
Nearby waterfall(s): Welsford Falls
Cellphone coverage: Y

Finding the trailhead: Drive south on Route 101, the road between Fredericton Junction and Welsford, looking for Ogden Road at 45°29'22.2" N, 66°26'59.8" W, just before the community of Clarendon. Drive straight out this logging road for 10.5 km to the trailhead on the left, just beyond the bridge over Sand Brook. The road is used for logging and, at times, can have deep ruts that make the drive a bit tricky.

Trailhead: 45°24'14.6" N, 66°29'31.6" W **Waterfall:** 45°24'13.7" N, 66°29'23.8" W

The hike: From the trailhead, follow the path as it meanders through the old-growth forest and makes for a pleasant hike to the waterfall. Near the crest of the ridge before the falls, the sound of the water permeates the forest canopy to welcome visitors. Sand Brook provides two falls for the enthusiast to enjoy. There is a path leading to the top of the first set of falls. To see the second falls, continue a bit further upstream. The finest location to view nature's handy-work is down the trail just below the first set of falls. From here, the small caves carved by the waterfall can be explored.

There are least four really nice waterfalls on Sand Brook throughout its run to the South Branch Oromocto River. Along the way, the brook meanders through forest and meadow, gathering the tannic acid from soil run off that gives it a brownish disposition.

Bonus feature(s): To explore the nearby bluffs at Bald Hill, referred to locally as Bald Mountain, simply turn off Ogden Road at 45°27'43.2" N, 66°28'49.1" W and drive roughly 2 km to the trailhead at 45°28'01.2" N, 66°30'16.0" W.

51. Mooneys Ridge Falls

TRUE
MAGNETIC

Contour Interval: 10M
500 METRES

Hampstead

Jerusalem Road

Spoon
Island

Saint John River

102

Fanning Brook

old
quarry

P

beaver
pond

Elevation

150

Mooneys
Ridge

10

Metres

35

Metres

413

20

Metres   100   200   300   400

51. Mooneys Ridge Falls

Type: Cascade
Height: 6 m
Best season(s): Spring, fall
Access: Trail, bushwhack
Source: Fanning Brook
Distance (one way): 413 m
Difficulty: Easy to moderate

Rating: 3
Hiking time: 20 minutes
Land ownership: Private
Map: NTS 021G09 Hampstead
Nearby waterfall(s): Welsford Falls, Henderson Falls
Cellphone coverage: Y

Finding the trailhead: Drive south on Route 102 from the village of Gagetown. The trailhead is on the west side of the road between Hampstead and Evandale. Look for the quarry entrance at 45°36'09.5" N, 66°04'14.1" W. Park at the entrance to the old quarry, which is located 4 km north of the access to the Evandale ferry. The trail is on the left side of the quarry.

Trailhead: 45°36'09.5" N, 66°04'14.1" W   **Waterfall:** 45°36'06.9" N, 66°04'30.3" W

The hike: The waterfall is nestled at the base of Mooneys Ridge, and there is no defined path leading to the falls. Follow the left edge of the quarry up and around to the back on the lookout, where there is an old path that leads through the woods to a large beaver pond. Do not be alarmed if the path does not become readily apparent — just continue heading in a northerly direction until you reach the beaver pond. Walk along the edge of it in an easterly direction to the brook that flows away from the pond down through the woods. Cross this brook and continue to hike along the edge of the pond until you reach a second brook that flows into the pond. Follow this brook into the woods to find the falls and an abandoned building made of Hampstead granite.

The falls are surrounded by beaver ponds and abandoned quarries that date back to the nineteenth century when this area supplied granite for buildings up and down the Wolastoq/Saint John River valley. In 1825, the quarry produced the granite blocks for Government House in Fredericton. The waterfall is unique in that it appears some of the granite blocks were placed strategically to channel the water to provide power for the old rock-cutting equipment.

52. Welsford Falls

Type: Fan
Height: 10 m
Best season(s): Spring, summer, fall
Access: Trail
Source: Welsford Falls Brook
Distance (one way): 342 m
Difficulty: Easy to moderate

Rating: 5
Hiking time: 20 minutes
Land ownership: Private
Map: NTS 021G08 Saint John
Nearby waterfall(s): Sand Brook Falls, Cunningham Creek Falls
Cellphone coverage: Y

Finding the trailhead: Drive south on Route 7 toward Saint John and take exit 63 to Welsford. At the intersection, turn left and then right on Route 101 North, driving toward the village and the intersection for Route 101 to Fredericton Junction. Turn right, drive approximately 1 km, and turn left at 45°27'27.5" N, 66°21'17.6" W onto a gravel access road, heading up into the hills behind the village. Drive to the bridge over Welsford Falls Brook. The trailhead is on the east side of the brook, just before the bridge.

52. Welsford Falls

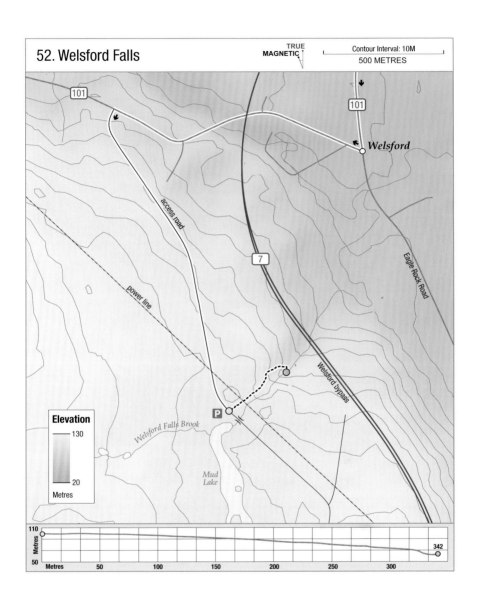

TRUE
MAGNETIC

Contour Interval: 10M
500 METRES

101

101

Welsford

access road

power line

7

Eagle Rock Road

Welsford bypass

P

Elevation
130

20
Metres

Welsford Falls Brook

Mud
Lake

110
Metres
50

Metres   50   100   150   200   250   300

342

52. Welsford Falls

Trailhead: 45°26'46.7" N, 66°20'54.9" W
Waterfall: 45°26'52.0" N, 66°20'44.0" W

The hike: To see this popular waterfall, simply follow the trail from the road into the woods and across a power line clearing. Keep to the trail as it follows the stream down to a clearing above the main falls. The entire area has stately tall pines, giving it a majestic atmosphere. From the apex of the trail, the view of the mountain to the east is wonderful.

Welsford Falls Brook tumbles down these steep hills, forming a series of three impressive waterfalls that drop over 30 m to the Nerepis River and, eventually, to the Wolastoq/ Saint John River. The most picturesque and photographed falls of the group is commonly known as Welsford Falls. At this juncture, the brook flows over the rock face, forming a stunning fan falls. Continuing downstream, the brook cuts a deep crevice in the bedrock, forming a precipitous gorge with ramparts rising 10 m to 20 m on either side. Through this particular section, a tiered waterfall with three drops twists and turns before emptying into a deep, narrow channel. Further downstream, beyond the new Welsford bypass, is a third waterfall. It cascades over rocky outcrops before smashing into a series of boulders strewn about the brook. The site is amazing, but the footing can be dangerous, and caution is urged as you make your way up and down the gorge.

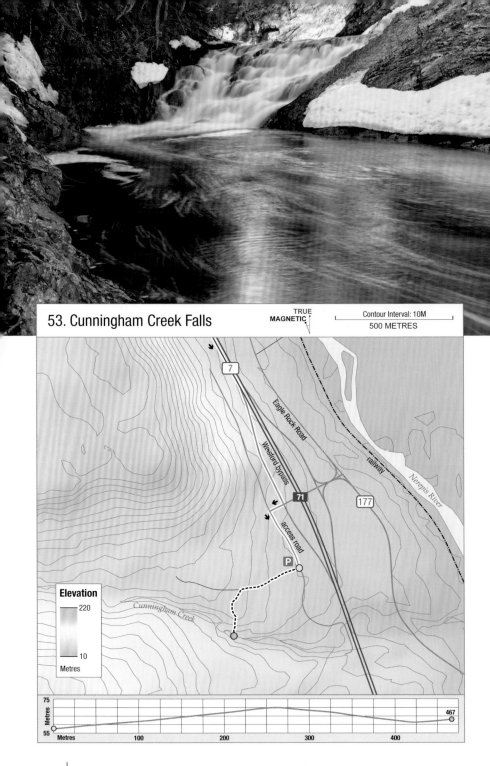

53. Cunningham Creek Falls

TRUE
MAGNETIC

Contour Interval: 10M
500 METRES

7

Eagle Rock Road

Welsford bypass

railway

Nerepis River

71

177

access road

P

Elevation

220

10

Metres

Cunningham Creek

75
Metres
55

467

Metres   100   200   300   400

53. Cunningham Creek Falls

Type: Cascade
Height: 8 m
Best season(s): Summer, fall
Access: Trail, bushwhack
Source: Cunningham Creek
Distance (one way): 467 m
Difficulty: Moderate to difficult

Rating: 3
Hiking time: 20 minutes
Land ownership: Private
Map: NTS 021G08 Saint John
Nearby waterfall(s): Sand Brook Falls, Welsford Falls
Cellphone coverage: Y

Finding the trailhead: Drive south on Route 7 toward Saint John. Near the end of the Welsford bypass, take exit 71 to Grand Bay-Westfield. At the intersection, turn right and then left onto the gravel access road. Drive roughly 150 m and park near the ATV trail on the right, being careful not to block the trail.

Trailhead: 45°24'06.0" N, 66°18'45.2" W   **Waterfall:** 45°23'57.0" N, 66°18'57.8" W

The hike: From the trailhead, follow the ATV trail north. After roughly 200 m, turn left into the woods and bushwhack through a stand of hardwoods. Within 100 m the trail descends into the ravine to a location just below the first set of waterfalls. This is a double-tiered waterfall, enclosed by 20 m rock walls. It is hard to photograph the two drops due to their twisted orientation. Cunningham Creek is one of several teeming watercourses tumbling their way down through the mountains to form the Nerepis River watershed. Over time, the creek has cut a narrow ravine through the hillside on its relentless journey to the sea.

Bonus fall(s): There are two sets of falls further up the creek. Backtrack to the ATV trail and follow the trail up the hill. The creek is on the left, and the sound of the cascades can be heard while hiking. The falls are at 45°24'03.7" N, 66°19'35.6" W and 45°24'02.9" N, 66°19'54.3" W.

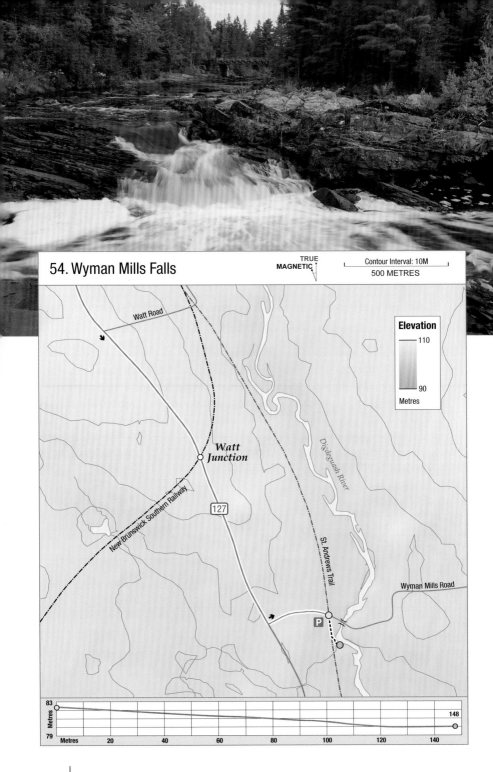

54. Wyman Mills Falls

TRUE
MAGNETIC

Contour Interval: 10M
500 METRES

Watt Road

Elevation
110
90
Metres

Watt Junction

Digdeguash River

New Brunswick Southern Railway

127

St. Andrews Trail

Wyman Mills Road

P

83
Metres
79
Metres 20 40 60 80 100 120 140
148

54. Wyman Mills Falls

Type: Slide
Height: 3 m
Best season(s): Spring, summer, fall
Access: Trail
Source: Digdeguash River
Distance (one way): 148 m
Difficulty: Easy

Rating: 2
Hiking time: 10 minutes
Land ownership: Crown
Map: NTS 021G06 St. George
Nearby waterfall(s): Saint Paddy's Falls
Cellphone coverage: N

Finding the trailhead: Head for St. Stephen on Route 3. Just beyond the stone train bridge at Lawrence Station, turn left on Route 127 toward Saint Andrews. Drive roughly 3.3 km, looking for the sign for Wyman Mills Road on the left. Drive 300 m on it and park along the roadside just before the bridge.

Trailhead: 45°24'02.1" N, 67°09'23.9" W   **Waterfall:** 45°23'57.8" N, 67°09'21.8" W

The hike: From the road, head south on the ATV trail down along the west side of the river. Near the waterfalls, there is a shortcut over the embankment to an excellent location to view the cascade and a bridge, located further upriver.

The Digdeguash River originates in a series of springs and wetlands near the village of McAdam and flows to the southeast before emptying into Passamaquoddy Bay. The river is relatively shallow and drifts over exposed bedrock. This combination produces many small waterfalls and much rough water throughout its length. The fall where Wyman Mills Road crosses the river is similar to others located further downstream. However, it stands out for its beautiful location where the river makes a left turn as it collides with a rockface along its western edge, slicing through the bedrock to form a slide. Beyond the falls, the river is strewn with boulders and widens as it continues to twist and turn on its journey. This area is a wonderful location to sit, contemplate, and enjoy life.

Bonus fall(s): Further along Route 127, there is a lovely set of rapids below the old train bridge on the Northwest Branch Digdeguash River at 45°23'03.1" N, 67°08'48.8" W.

FUNDY COASTAL DRIVE

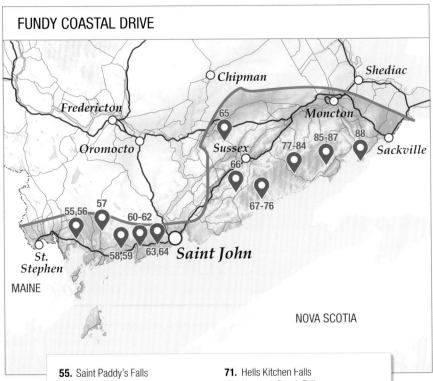

55. Saint Paddy's Falls	**71.** Hells Kitchen Falls
56. Hidden Falls	**72.** Hemlock Brook Falls
57. Red Rock Stream Falls	**73.** Bonnell Brook Falls
58. Knights Mill Brook Falls	**74.** Parlee Brook Falls
59. New River Falls	**75.** Long Beach Brook Falls
60. Keyhole Falls	**76.** Walton Glen Brook Falls
61. Little Lepreau River Falls	**77.** Wallace Falls
62. Moose Creek Falls	**78.** Tweedledum and Tweedledee Falls
63. First Falls, West Branch Musquash River	**79.** Goose Creek Falls
64. Perch Brook Falls	**80.** Sproul Settlement Falls
65. Kierstead Mountain Falls	**81.** Pollett River Falls
66. Back Settlement Road Falls	**82.** East Branch Point Wolfe River Falls
67. First Falls, Porter Brook (Saint John)	**83.** Haley Brook Falls
68. Big Rody Brook Falls	**84.** Upper Falls, Third Vault Brook
69. Little Rody Brook Falls	**85.** Beaver Brook Falls
70. Pine Brook Falls	**86.** Bough Brook Falls
	87. Midway Falls
	88. Slacks Cove Falls

Fundy Coastal Drive

Writing in the 1800s, the renowned geologist and naturalist Abraham Gesner called the scenery of the Fundy Coast "wild and picturesque." With everything from rugged mountain scenes to dramatic seascapes, in a region cooled in summer and warmed in winter by the Bay of Fundy, the Fundy Coastal Drive's natural beauty continues to attract naturalists and waterfall enthusiasts alike. Stretching from St. Stephen in the west to Aulac in the east, it is divided into two regions by the Wolastoq/Saint John River.

The Fundy Coastal Drive follows the bay from St. Stephen to Saint John, passing quaint fishing communities and beautiful ocean vistas. As you drive along this section, you will see several waterfalls from the roadside. William Francis Ganong, in his physiographic study of the bay, noted that all the rivers west of and including the Wolastoq/Saint John River enter the Bay of Fundy by flowing over a waterfall. The rivers in this area are low and rocky with glacial debris blocking their original paths. Keyhole Falls and Little Lepreau River Falls are fine examples.

61. Lepreau Falls (bonus fall)

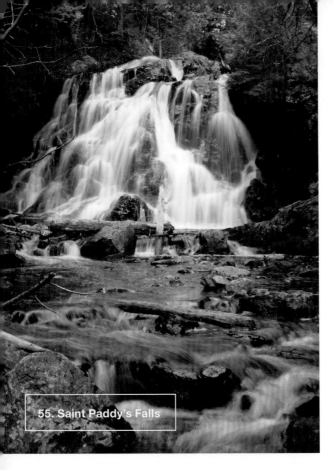

55. Saint Paddy's Falls

In contrast, the rivers in the region east of Saint John enter the Bay of Fundy through steep-sided estuaries. The many rivers and brooks were not disrupted to the same extent over the eons as the glacial rivers to the west and flow through narrow valleys. This region — which includes the Caledonia Highlands, with some of the oldest geology in the world — is now part of the Stonehammer UNESCO Global Geopark. It is dominated by windswept mountains and is greatly affected by the moist air from the Bay. There are fewer communities remaining along this rugged coast. Starting just up the road from the coastal village of St. Martins, the Fundy Trail Parkway has expanded eastward to connect with a road leading to Sussex, only 30 km from Fundy National Park, opening up the Caledonia Highlands to waterfall and nature enthusiasts. Some of New Brunswick's highest waterfalls, such as Walton Glen Brook Falls, are found in the highlands southeast of Sussex. Because of the rough terrain, the scenic route veers inland in two areas, following the Kennebecasis River valley and then along the Petitcodiac River.

76. Walton Glen Gorge Falls

55. Saint Paddy's Falls

Type: Fan
Height: 6 m
Best season(s): Spring, fall
Access: Trail
Source: Unidentified
Distance (one way): 425 m
Difficulty: Easy

Rating: 4
Hiking time: 20 minutes
Land ownership: Private
Map: NTS 021G03 St. Stephen
Nearby waterfall(s): Hidden Falls
Cellphone coverage: Y

Finding the trailhead: Drive west on Route 1 toward St. Stephen and take exit 39 (Bocabec/Saint Andrews) to Route 127. At the intersection, turn right onto Basin Road and then immediately take a left onto Basin Access Road. Drive approximately 2.6 km to the intersection with Kerrs Ridge Road. Stay right and follow Kerrs Ridge Road a further 325 m. Drive slowly, on the lookout for

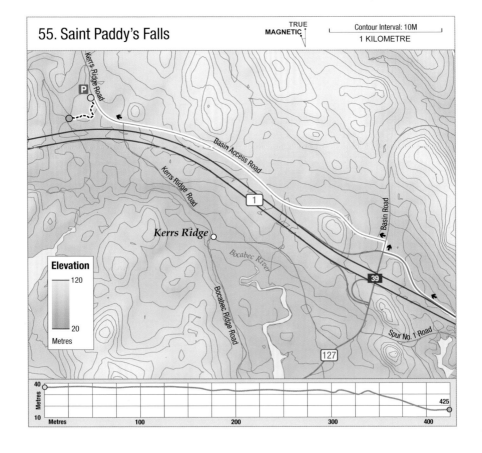

the trailhead near a utility pole at the treeline on the left. There is a sign at the trailhead. Turn and park beyond the guardrails as this is a busy road.

Trailhead: 45°12'09.3" N, 67°00'33.0" W   **Waterfall:** 45°12'03.8" N, 67°00'43.0" W

The hike: The well-trodden trail is an indication of the popularity of the area. The unnamed brook originates from Kerrs Lake and the wetlands along the eastern edge of Kerrs Ridge, and it pours down over the rock face to produce a beautiful waterfall. Locally known as Saint Paddy's, the falls are easily accessible by both young and old. From the trailhead, the footpath meanders through a lush forest covered with emerald green moss. At times the path circles around boulders and rocky outcrops as it tracks the ridge in a sweep westward to the brook and waterfall. The trail eventually arrives at a large open area, inviting visitors to enjoy the spectacular waterfall, spilling over the edge of the rock face. Once down in the bowl, the uniqueness of this waterfall becomes very apparent. Graced by an overstorey of mixed hardwood and softwood, it captivates its audience as it flows majestically and gently across the rock face, producing a veil of white water.

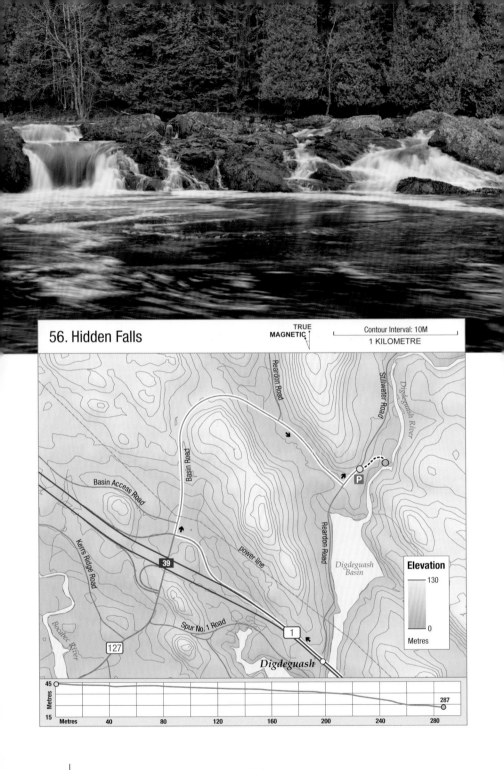

56. Hidden Falls

TRUE
MAGNETIC

Contour Interval: 10M
1 KILOMETRE

56. Hidden Falls

Type: Cascade
Height: 5 m
Best season(s): Spring, fall
Access: Trail, bushwhack
Source: Digdeguash River
Distance (one way): 287 m
Difficulty: Easy to moderate

Rating: 2
Hiking time: 20 minutes
Land ownership: Private
Map: NTS 021G02 St. George
Nearby waterfall(s): Saint Paddy's Falls
Cellphone coverage: Y

Finding the trailhead: Drive west on Route 1 toward St. Stephen and take exit 39 (Bocabec/Saint Andrews) to Route 127. Turn right at the intersection onto Basin Road and follow the road for 2.6 km to the end where it intersects with Stillwater Road. Turn left and drive approximately 100 m up the road. There is an old woods road on the right, leading down toward the river. Pull safely off Stillwater Road and park.

Trailhead: 45°11'43.0" N, 66°57'28.8" W   **Waterfall:** 45°11'44.6" N, 66°57'18.4" W

The hike: There are several names circulating for this waterfall. Without any documentation, I used the most familiar. Throughout its length, the woods road is dry until a number of natural streams bubble up near the bottom, making this section very wet even during the hottest months of the summer. Near the bottom of the road, the sound of the waterfall can be heard, so be on the lookout for the trail leading on a direct trajectory to the falls. If all else fails, just head for the river and the sound. This waterfall spans the entire width of the Digdeguash River. The location is an excellent place to escape the mid-summer heat. The site is impressive when embraced by late summer wildflowers or the hues of autumn colours. For the historian, there are remnants of an old mill or dam remaining along the west side of the falls.

Bonus fall(s): Located at the Digdeguash Basin at 45°11'29.9" N, 66°57'25.7" W is another of those waterfalls that change due to the phenomenal Bay of Fundy tides.

57. Red Rock Stream Falls

Type: Slide
Height: 3 m
Best season(s): Spring, fall
Access: Trail
Source: Unidentified
Distance (one way): 101 m
Difficulty: Easy

Rating: 2
Hiking time: 10 minutes
Land ownership: Crown
Map: NTS 021G07 McDougall Lake
Nearby waterfall(s): New River Falls
Cellphone coverage: Y

Finding the trailhead: Head west on Route 1 from Saint John. Take exit 60 to Lake Utopia, turn right at the end of the exit ramp, and then turn left onto Route 785 North. Drive for roughly 16 km on the lookout for Red Rock Road. Turn right onto the gravel road opposite it and drive approximately 1.2 km beside blueberry fields. The road eventually opens onto a clearing with a Maritimes & Northeast Pipeline right-of-way on the left. Drive along the right-of-way and park near the woods.

57. Red Rock Stream Falls

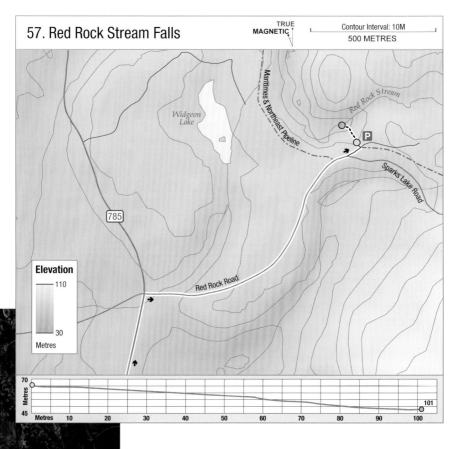

Trailhead: 45°14'58.1" N, 66°45'40.7" W **Waterfall:** 45°15'00.4" N, 66°45'43.1" W

The hike: The trailhead is not hard to find. From the clearing, follow the path through the woods directly to the waterfall. For the most part, the stream draining Red Rock Lake wanders effortlessly toward the Magaguadavic River, except here where it trundles over the shoulder of Red Rock Ridge. The ridge divides the stream into various paths before they rejoin further down. Above the main cascade are a series of smaller falls, making for a wonderful photographic experience, especially in autumn.

58. Knights Mill Brook Falls

Type: Tiered
Height: 4 m
Best season(s): Spring, fall
Access: Roadside, trail
Source: Knights Mill Brook
Distance (one way): 1.3 km
Difficulty: Easy

Rating: 3
Hiking time: 40 minutes
Land ownership: Crown
Map: NTS 021G02 St. George
Nearby waterfall(s): New River Falls
Cellphone coverage: Y

Finding the trailhead: From Saint John, drive west on Route 1 to exit 69 for Pennfield and Pocologan. Pull well off the roadway and park near the highway sign. The trailhead begins at the nearby deer gate on the right.

Trailhead: 45°7'19.1" N, 66°37'53.5" W   **Waterfall:** 45°7'37.3" N, 66°37'21.1" W

The hike: Push through the deer gate and start hiking east (to the right) on the logging road. This is a pleasant walk, especially in autumn. Look for the trail on the right, just before the wooden bridge spanning the brook. There are two

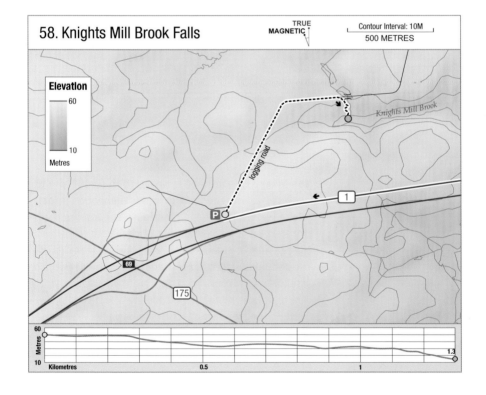

58. Knights Mill Brook Falls

waterfalls for the enthusiast to enjoy, both very photogenic. It is a short hike as the trail swings down along the west side of the brook to the upper tier falls. Continue on the trail to the right, away from the brook, and it will swing back to a level area at the bottom of the larger second waterfall.

The brook was named for Joshua Knight, a Pennsylvania Loyalist who was granted the original land grant. Much like other watercourses in this part of the province, Knights Mill Brook has its origin in many small ponds and wetlands. On its slow meander to Crow Harbour and the Bay of Fundy, the brook gathers tannic acid from decaying flora, turning the water a light shade of brown.

59. New River Falls

Type: Cascade
Height: 4 m
Best season(s): Spring, fall
Access: Trail
Source: New River
Distance (one way): 174 m
Difficulty: Easy

Rating: 3
Hiking time: 20 minutes
Land ownership: Crown
Map: NTS 021G02 St. George
Nearby waterfall(s): Keyhole Falls
Cellphone coverage: Y

Finding the trailhead: Drive west from Saint John along Route 1 and take exit 86 for Lepreau. At the intersection, turn left and head south on Route 790 toward Lepreau, then turn right onto Route 175. Drive west through the village toward New River and turn right at 45°09'55.1" N, 66°28'35.9" W onto Route 780, known locally as Old Saint John Road. Drive roughly 5.7 km to the trailhead, just before the bridge over New River, and park alongside the road. The trailhead is where the ATV trail meets the road.

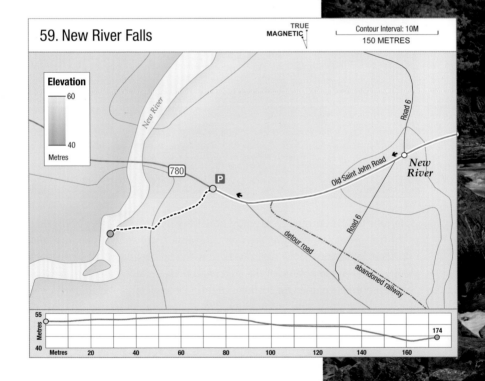

Trailhead: 45°10'34.0" N, 66°32'30.2" W   **Waterfall:** 45°10'32.0" N, 66°32'37.1" W

The hike: This is a fairly easy waterfall for young to old enthusiasts to visit because of the relative flatness of the land with no deep valleys. From the road, simply follow the ATV trail southward for roughly 180 m through the woods to a clearing next to the top of the cascade. It is a popular location as the flat rocks along the edge provide an excellent location to sit and enjoy the waterfall and the surroundings. Bring along a picnic and enjoy a bit of wilderness. There are several waterfalls on New River between its headwaters at Ormond Lake and New River Beach Provincial Park at the mouth. Typical of the rock-bound rivers in this area, New River cascades directly into the Bay of Fundy.

Bonus fall(s): Further downstream, there are numerous cascades with two that are noteworthy to explore at 45°10'05.3" N, 66°32'45.7" W and 45°09'37.1" N, 66°32'45.1" W.

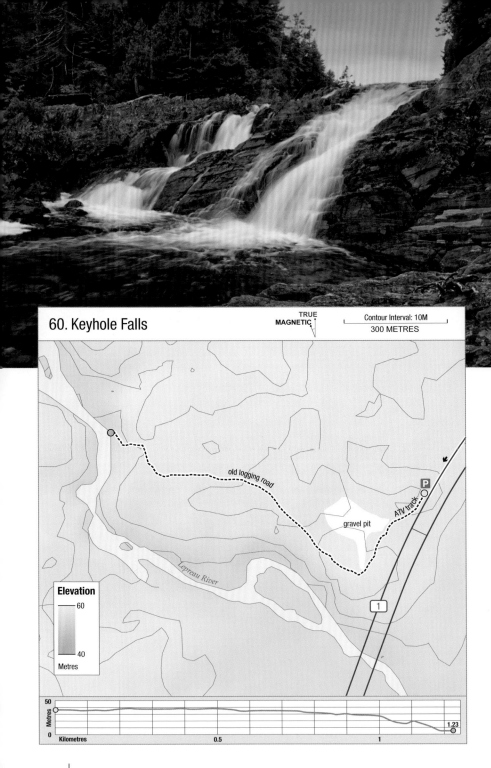

60. Keyhole Falls

TRUE
MAGNETIC

Contour Interval: 10M
300 METRES

old logging road

P

ATV track

gravel pit

Lepreau River

1

Elevation

60

40

Metres

50

Metres

0

Kilometres

0.5

1

1.23

60. Keyhole Falls

Type: Tiered
Height: 6 m
Best season(s): Summer, fall
Access: Trail
Source: Lepreau River
Distance (one way): 1.2 km
Difficulty: Easy to moderate

Rating: 5
Hiking time: 40 minutes
Land ownership: Crown
Map: NTS 021G01 Musquash
Nearby waterfall(s): Little Lepreau River Falls
Cellphone coverage: Y

Finding the trailhead: Drive west from Saint John along Route 1 and pull off the highway just before reaching the bridge over the Lepreau River. The trailhead is at the deer gate on the right at the top of the embankment.

Trailhead: 45°10'47.1" N, 66°28'45.8" W **Waterfall:** 45°10'53.0" N, 66°29'27.5" W

The hike: Hike up the embankment and go through the deer gate. Follow the ATV track westward into a gravel pit. Stay to the left and hike around the pit until reaching the old logging road. Follow the road along the brow of the eastern ridge that forms the Lepreau River valley. The hike along the road through the forest is enjoyable as the sound of the highway slowly dissipates and the sound of the waterfall begins to permeate up through the forest canopy. Roughly 50 m after crossing a small stream, look for the marking tape indicating the route down the embankment to the river, emerging just below the bottom falls. Concealed from view, the upper falls are in a sharp notch in the bedrock, and it is no wonder the waterfall is called Keyhole. The power of the river found a weakness in the formation and carved deeply into the rock. This section must be thunderous during the spring freshet.

The impressive Keyhole Falls are a combination of two distinct falls in a unique geological formation where the exposed bedrock is oriented both vertically and horizontally. The formation contains several strata of different rock of which one band is quartz, forming a white ribbon across the riverbed. The erosive power of the last ice age, in combination with the incessant wear by the river, has exposed the volcanic fissures or dikes. Take time to examine the evidence of the forces of nature that produced this unique location.

61. Little Lepreau River Falls

Type: Cascade
Height: 3 m
Best season(s): Spring, summer, fall
Access: Trail
Source: Little Lepreau Brook
Distance (one way): 99 m
Difficulty: Easy

Rating: 2
Hiking time: 10 minutes
Land ownership: Crown
Map: NTS 021G01 Musquash
Nearby waterfall(s): Keyhole Falls
Cellphone coverage: Y

Finding the trailhead: From Saint John, drive west on Route 1 and take exit 86 to Route 790 to Lepreau. At the intersection, turn left and drive south toward Maces Bay for 6.5 km, watching for Little Lepreau Road on the right. Turn onto this road and drive approximately 500 m to the waterfall. Just past the guardrail on the right, there is a parking area.

Trailhead: 45°08'03.6" N, 66°27'39.5" W
Waterfall: 45°08'2.3" N, 66°27'36.9" W

The hike: The trailhead begins in the parking area. Walk back across the road, climb over the guardrail, and scramble down to the waterfall. Similar to all the rivers west of Saint John, this is a waterfall within the tidal zone, and the best time to see the falls is at low tide. The river cascades into the Little Lepreau Basin, where fresh and salt waters mix. It is also where cool breezes and fog are pushed up the inlet as the tide begins to rise. The low buffering capacity of bogs and wetlands is not uncommon throughout the watershed, so these areas tend to be naturally acidic. This condition readily leaches iron and other minerals from the soil, turning the water a caramel colour.

Thanks to the foresight of government engineers, an added attraction is the Little Lepreau Covered Bridge, which was moved to its present location to make way for road improvements. Take time to visit the bridge and the tranquil water just above it. The entire area is striking when draped in autumn colours. The name Lepreau is of French origin and is a derivative of *lapereau*, meaning "little rabbit." The current spelling has existed since the mid-nineteenth century.

Bonus fall: Nearby Lepreau Falls is a ten minute drive away at the following coordinates: 45°10'09.8" N, 66°27'41.1" W

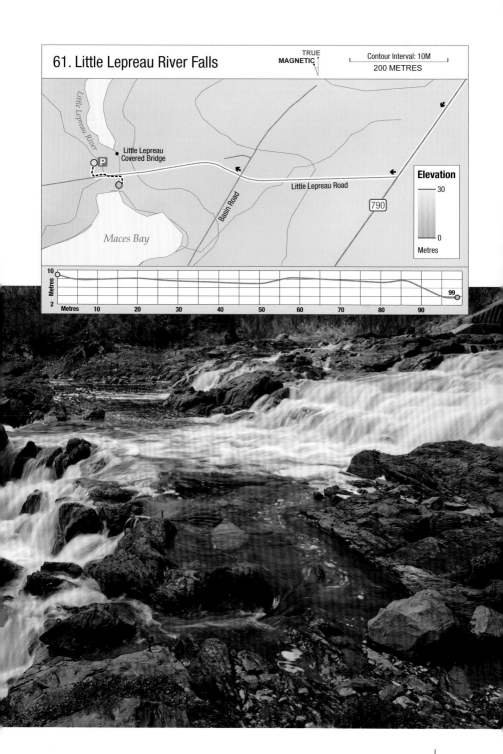

61. Little Lepreau River Falls

TRUE
MAGNETIC

Contour Interval: 10M
200 METRES

Little Lepreau River

Little Lepreau
Covered Bridge

P

Basin Road

Little Lepreau Road

790

Elevation

30

0

Metres

Maces Bay

10
Metres
2

Metres   10   20   30   40   50   60   70   80   90

99

62. Moose Creek Falls

TRUE
MAGNETIC

Contour Interval: 10M
1 KILOMETRES

Elevation

— 50

0

Metres

Chance Harbour

Moose Creek

790

Chance Harbour Road

Little Dipper Harbour

Cemetery Loop Road

P

Bay of Fundy

18

12

Metres

727

Metres   100   200   300   400   500   600   700

62. Moose Creek Falls

Type: Cascade
Height: 3 m
Best season(s): Spring, fall
Access: Trail, bushwhack
Source: Moose Creek
Distance (one way): 727 m
Difficulty: Easy to moderate

Rating: 3
Hiking time: 20 minutes
Land ownership: Crown
Map: NTS 021G01 Musquash
Nearby waterfall(s): First Falls, West Branch Musquash River
Cellphone coverage: Y

Finding the trailhead: From Saint John, drive west along Route 1 and take exit 96 to Musquash and Chance Harbour. Turn left at the intersection onto Route 790 and head for Chance Harbour. Follow Route 790 for 12.5 km to the trailhead and park alongside the road.

Trailhead: 45°06'53.0" N, 66°22'58.8" W **Waterfall:** 45°07'12.1" N, 66°22'59.7" W

The hike: From the highway, hike the woods road through an old clearcut, which is beginning to regrow, until reaching the bridge across the creek. The road is also used by ATV enthusiasts, so be aware of their presence. Immediately after the crossing the bridge, turn right, cross the shallow ditch, and hike into the woods. Follow the path 30 m or so down along the creek to the estuary, where it becomes rather steep. Once in the estuary, follow the edge of the salt grass and exposed bedrock to the best location to view the falls.

At extreme high tides, walking along the edge of the salt grass is impossible. Therefore, consult the tide tables before visiting this area of the Bay of Fundy. The estuary is very appealing and wondrous in its own right, especially at dusk. The creek begins at Retreat Lake and gingerly flows through a series of wetlands until cascading into the Moose Creek estuary and, further yet, to Little Dipper Harbour on the bay.

63. First Falls, West Branch Musquash River

TRUE
MAGNETIC

Contour Interval: 10M
250 METRES

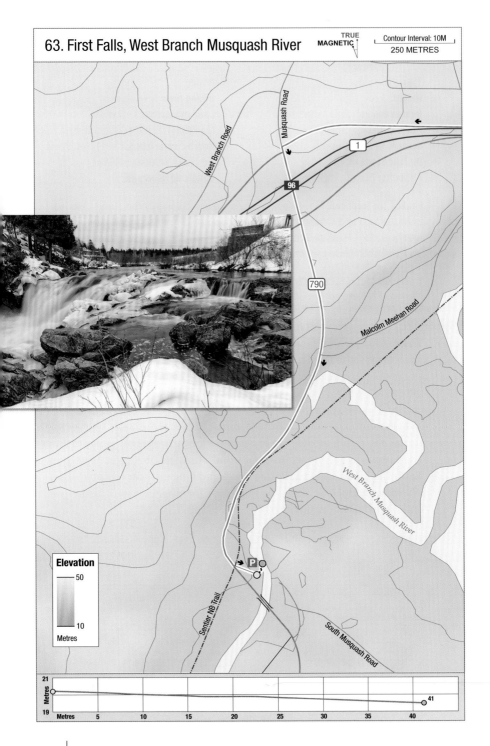

West Branch Road

Musquash Road

1

96

790

Malcolm Meehan Road

West Branch Musquash River

Elevation

— 50

— 10

Metres

Sentier NB Trail

P

South Musquash Road

21
Metres
19
| Metres | 5 | 10 | 15 | 20 | 25 | 30 | 35 | 40 |

41

63. First Falls, West Branch Musquash River

Type: Cascade
Height: 5 m
Best season(s): Year-round
Access: Trail
Source: West Branch Musquash River
Distance (one way): 41 m
Difficulty: Easy

Rating: 2
Hiking time: 5 minutes
Land ownership: Crown
Map: NTS 021G01 Musquash
Nearby waterfall(s): Perch Brook Falls, Moose Creek Falls
Cellphone coverage: Y

Finding the trailhead: From Saint John, drive west along Route 1 and take exit 96 to Musquash and Chance Harbour. At the intersection, turn left onto Route 790 and head for Chance Harbour. Drive about 1.5 km and take the access road on the left just before the bridge over the West Branch Musquash River. Drive 100 m to the trailhead. There are a viewing platform and a picnic table at the old bridge abutment.

Trailhead: 45°10'48.8" N, 66°20'25.0" W **Waterfall:** 45°10'49.7" N, 66°20'23.8" W

The hike: It is a short walk along the trail to the rock outcrops below the waterfall. The West Branch Musquash River features a variety of waterfalls, all located between the dam and the point at which the river drops into the estuary, and all are worth seeing. Take time to watch the tides flood back up through the estuary to the waterfall, changing its character. The Musquash River estuary has been designated a national Marine Protected Area; more recently, Loch Alva, located at the head of the river, was named a provincial Protected Natural Area. The two designations combine to preserve this watershed, from the headwaters to the Bay of Fundy. There are three additional waterfalls to explore in the vicinity, as well as Scott Falls Dam.

Bonus fall(s): There are three notable waterfalls to visit while in the area. Two on the West Branch Musquash are at the following coordinates: 45°11'07.2" N, 66°21'18.2" W and 45°11'04.4" N, 66°21'08.2" W. There is another waterfall on the East Branch Musquash River at 45°11'51.5" N, 66°19'31.1" W, where the hydro dam has been decommissioned.

64. Perch Brook Falls

Type: Tiered

Height: 3 m

Best season(s): Spring, fall

Access: Trail

Source: Perch Brook

Distance (one way): 48 m

Difficulty: Easy

Rating: 2

Hiking time: 5 minutes

Land ownership: Crown

Map: NTS 021G01 Musquash

Nearby waterfall(s): First Falls, West Branch Musquash River

Cellphone coverage: Y

Finding the trailhead: Drive west on Route 1 from Saint John and take exit 103 to Prince of Wales. At the end of the exit, continue straight on Shadow Lake Road. After a large culvert for the brook there is a pond on the right and just beyond a rock cut. Just after the cut there is a trail that leads to the falls.

Note: After rain, the trail becomes very slippery.

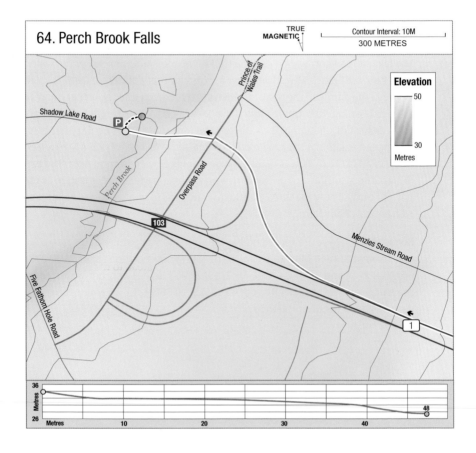

Trailhead: 45°12'24.8" N, 66°16'05.2" W **Waterfall:** 45°12'25.6" N, 66°16'03.6" W

The hike: From the trailhead, follow the short path through the spruce and tamarack trees to the waterfall, which is nestled in the woods a short distance from the service road. Here, a few kilometres upriver from its confluence with the Musquash River estuary, Perch Brook begins its descent by cutting through a gap in the ridge that is the division between the plateau and the estuary. This is very noticeable when driving downhill from the plateau to the broad estuary along Route 1. With its beginnings in Perch Lake, the diminutive brook meanders through a narrow dale along the nape of Marshall Mountain and eventually becomes a wonderful little waterfall and pool within the narrow ravine. This easily accessible waterfall provides a respite from the hustle and bustle of our self-imposed schedules.

65. Kierstead Mountain Falls

TRUE
MAGNETIC

Contour Interval: 10M
500 METRES

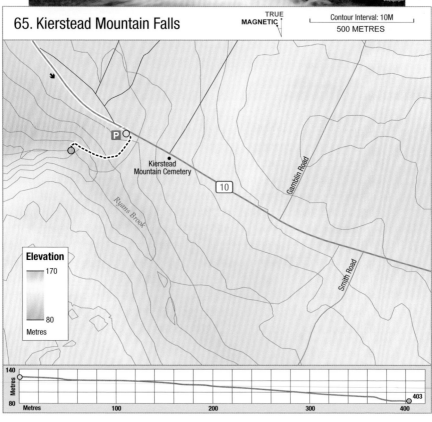

Kierstead
Mountain Cemetery

10

Gamblin Road

Smith Road

Ryans Brook

Elevation
170

80
Metres

140
Metres
80   Metres   100   200   300   400

403

65. Kierstead Mountain Falls

Type: Cascade
Height: 8 m
Best season(s): Spring, fall
Access: Trail
Source: Big Brook
Distance (one way): 403 m
Difficulty: Easy to moderate

Rating: 3
Hiking time: 20 minutes
Land ownership: Private
Map: NTS 021H13 Codys
Nearby waterfall(s): Beatty Brook Falls (Kings)
Cellphone coverage: Y

Finding the trailhead: From Coles Island, drive on Route 10 toward Sussex. About 200 m before the Kierstead Mountain Cemetery on the right — there is only one graveyard along this stretch of road, so it is hard to miss — there is a guardrail on the right. Next to it is a road leading down to a small clearing where an old logging road is the trail. In spring and autumn, the grassy clearing becomes very slippery, so I suggest parking up along the main highway.

Trailhead: 45°50'12.1" N, 65°42'44.6" W   **Waterfall:** 45°50'09.7" N, 65°42'56.8" W

The hike: Follow the old logging road for approximately 225 m to the trail on the left, leading down to the base of the waterfall. The sound of the falls will provide guidance. The hike through the woods on the old logging road is very pleasant as it descends away from the sound of the highway. In spring, the old road is very wet and muddy, and in autumn, it is alive with colour.

This is a pretty little waterfall that would be easy for small children to walk to with guidance. The brook has carved the left side of the ravine, forming an indentation in the bedrock. Similar to other waterfalls without a permanent source, such as a lake, it dries to just a trickle during a hot, dry summer. Scattered in the ravine are remnants of an old mill, possibly washed down by the torrential spring freshets. One neat thing about waterfalling is the discovery of old mill equipment, old homesteads, and the family apple trees that are now growing wild.

66. Back Settlement Road Falls

Type: Fan

Height: 4 m

Best season(s): Spring, fall

Access: Trail

Source: Scoodic Brook

Distance (one way): 314 m

Difficulty: Easy

Rating: 4

Hiking time: 20 minutes

Land ownership: Crown

Map: NTS 021H12 Sussex

Nearby waterfall(s): Ratcliffe Brook Falls

Cellphone coverage: N

Finding the trailhead: From the Saint John Airport, drive east on Route 111 toward St. Martins and take the exit for Route 820, also known as Barnesville Road, and the rural community of Upham. Drive roughly 26.5 km to the access road at 45°29'28.1" N, 65°39'12.0" W. In Upham, turn left and drive up Robinson Road around 1.5 km and turn right onto Back Settlement Road. Take this gravel road and drive 4 km to the trailhead. Park alongside the road. There is a surprising amount of traffic for a woods road, and it is extremely muddy in early spring.

Trailhead: 45°31'10.3" N, 65°36'36.6" W **Waterfall:** 45°31'16.0" N, 65°36'33.2" W

The hike: From Back Settlement Road, follow the ATV trail for about 300 m. The hike into the falls is through a very pleasant archway of trees. If the water is low, cross the brook near the top of the falls where a well-groomed pathway on the left leads down into the ravine. If there is too much water, use the rougher path just before the brook to descend to the waterfall. Back Settlement Road Falls is tucked behind McShane Hill and is on Scoodic Brook. Nestled in the Hammond River valley, the falls are small but beautiful as the brook drops in three sections over the face of the conglomerate rock through lush emerald vegetation on its journey to the Hammond River. It is quiet in the small ravine. Large pine and fir trees, mixed with an overstorey of hardwood, make for a relaxed atmosphere.

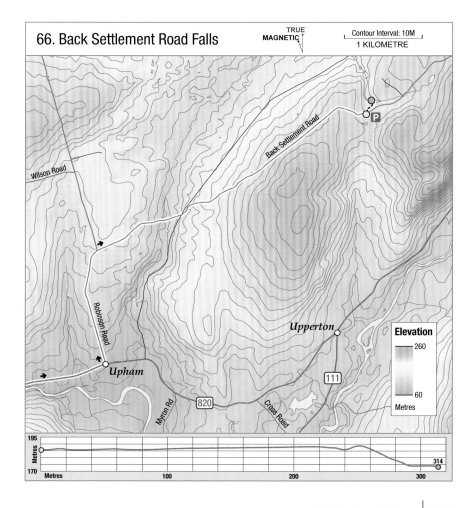

67. First Falls, Porter Brook (Saint John)

Type: Drop
Height: 10 m
Best season(s): Spring, fall
Access: Trail, bushwhack
Source: McFadden Lake
Distance (one way): 2.6 km
Difficulty: Moderate to difficult

Rating: 4
Hiking time: 2 hours
Land ownership: Crown
Map: NTS 021H06 Salmon River
Nearby waterfall(s): Big Rody Brook Falls, Little Rody Brook Falls
Cellphone coverage: N

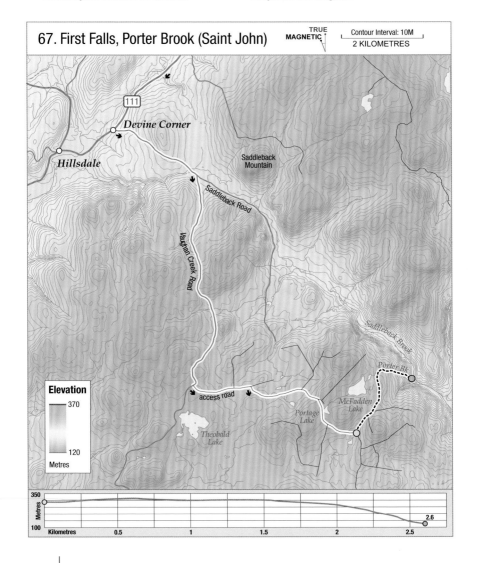

67. First Falls, Porter Brook (Saint John)

Finding the trailhead: From Sussex Corner, head for St. Martins on Route 111. Drive to the turnoff to Saddleback Road at coordinates 45°32'39.3" N, 65°32'36.2" W. Drive out the gravel road approximately 2.5 km to the junction with Vaughan Creek Road. Note: there is an old cemetery on the right. Turn right onto Vaughan Creek Road and drive about 5.5 km to coordinates 45°29'18.6" N, 65°31'10.8" W. Turn left and drive out the access road 1.5 km and turn right. Continue past Portage Lake, located on the left of the access road. There are a few areas where the road is a bit rough, yet passable for a vehicle with good clearance.

Trailhead: 45°28'39.6" N, 65°28'08.2" W   **Waterfall:** 45°29'21.5" N, 65°27'06.3" W

The hike: Hike up the old logging road to the road on the left. Follow this road for roughly 1 km until reaching Porter Brook. The old road has grown in a bit but is very manageable. Just before reaching an old and dilapidated logging bridge over the brook, turn right and begin a bushwhack descent along the brook. Within minutes, the first of several waterfalls will attract your attention.

Continue to the stated coordinates, where the highest and finest of the waterfalls is located just before the confluence with Saddleback Brook.

With its headwaters in the boggy meadows of Portage Lake and McFadden Lake, Porter Brook tumbles down the side of the hill. In comparison, falls like Big and Little Rody have cut deep ravines into the landscape. Much of the surrounding forest has been harvested in recent years, except for a narrow corridor of trees that shade the brook from sunlight. This is a particularly beautiful area when draped in autumn colours.

68. Big Rody Brook Falls

TRUE
MAGNETIC

Contour Interval: 10M
2 KILOMETRES

Elevation

— 350

— 50

Metres

Little Rody Brook

P

Vaughan Creek Road

logging road

Big Rody Brook

160

Metres

40

Metres

100

200

300

400

500

567

68. Big Rody Brook Falls

Type: Drop
Height: 5 m
Best season(s): Spring, summer, fall
Access: Bushwhack
Source: Big Rody Brook
Distance (one way): 567 m
Difficulty: Difficult to extreme

Rating: 5
Hiking time: 40 minutes
Land ownership: Crown
Map: NTS 021H06 Salmon River
Nearby waterfall(s): Little Rody Falls, First Falls, Porter Brook (Saint John)
Cellphone coverage: N

Finding the trailhead: Drive along Main Street through the village of St. Martins. At the Y intersection with Big Salmon River Road, go left on Vaughan Creek Road. Drive approximately 9 km as it turns from asphalt to gravel to 45°25'56.1" N, 65°31'30.4" W. Turn right onto the logging road and drive 9.7 km turning right at 45°27'02.9" N, 65°26'15.2" W. Turn left at 45°26'11.8" N, 65°26'34.6" W and continue to the trailhead at the end of the road.
Note: These rough roads require a vehicle with good clearance and tires.

Trailhead: 45°26'08.5" N, 65°26'10.8" W   **Waterfall:** 45°26'08.7" N, 65°25'56.9" W

The hike: Please note that this hike is rated difficult to extreme and is not for the faint of heart. Big Rody is a tremendous natural wilderness area that must be seen to be appreciated. From the trailhead, bushwhack down the steep ravine through a dense forest to the first of several waterfalls. The brook changes quickly from its meager beginnings at Rody Lake to a turbulent watercourse that drops more than 152 m over 5 km through the Caledonia Highlands. The gorge has sheer cliffs that rise well over 25 m, making access tricky. Stately mature pine trees along the edges of the brook give the area a wild and magnificent appearance. I have been into the Big Rody on two occasions, and on both, I was overwhelmed by its rugged beauty.

Bonus fall(s): The two waterfalls upstream at 45°26'04.4" N, 65°25'56.9" W and 45°25'59.3" N, 65°26'19.1" W require a circuitous and difficult hike of 1.5 km, climbing over rocks and grappling with tree roots.

68. Big Rody Brook Falls

69. Little Rody Brook Falls

TRUE
MAGNETIC

Contour Interval: 10M
2 KILOMETRES

Little Rody Brook

Elevation

350

50

Metres

P

Vaughan Creek Road

logging road

Big Rody Brook

200

Metres

80

100   200   300   400

431

Metres

69. Little Rody Brook Falls

Type: Drop
Height: 4 m
Best season(s): Spring, summer, fall
Access: Bushwhack
Source: Little Rody Brook
Distance (one way): 431 m
Difficulty: Difficult to extreme

Rating: 5
Hiking time: 40 minutes
Land ownership: Crown
Map: NTS 021H06 Salmon River
Nearby waterfall(s): Big Rody Falls; First Falls, Porter Brook (Saint John)
Cellphone coverage: N

Finding the trailhead: Drive along Main Street through the village of St. Martins. At the Y intersection with Big Salmon River Road, go left on Vaughan Creek Road as it turns from asphalt to gravel. Drive approximately 9 km to coordinates 45°25'56.1" N, 65°31'30.4" W. Turn right onto the logging road and drive 7.4 km to the trailhead, and park along the roadside.
Note: These roads are sparsely maintained and require a vehicle with good clearance and tires.

Trailhead: 45°27'04.3" N, 65°26'18.9" W **Waterfall:** 45 27'09.8" N, 65 26'09.5" W

The hike: Please note that this hike is rated difficult to extreme and will require hiking down a steep-sided gorge. From the trailhead, bushwhack across a clearcut and then down the steep ravine. The coordinates above lead to the second in a series of falls within the gorge. Remnants still remain there of a "rolling dam" from bygone logging operations, which had been placed over the waterfall to help the passage of logs during the spring river drive. The little brother to Big Rody Brook is another of the turbulent watercourses in the Caledonia Highlands. In its short and raucous run, Little Rody Brook has several waterfalls, two of which are simply outstanding. The gorge contains sheer cliffs that tower above each of the falls, making access exciting. This whole area is wild and magnificent with old-growth forest shading the ravine.

Bonus fall(s): There are falls downstream and upstream to explore, but extreme hiking is required to climb around the rock outcrops. The coordinates for two of the worthier falls are 45°27'18.9" N, 65°26'20.6" W and 45° 27'23.1" N, 65°26'30.6" W.

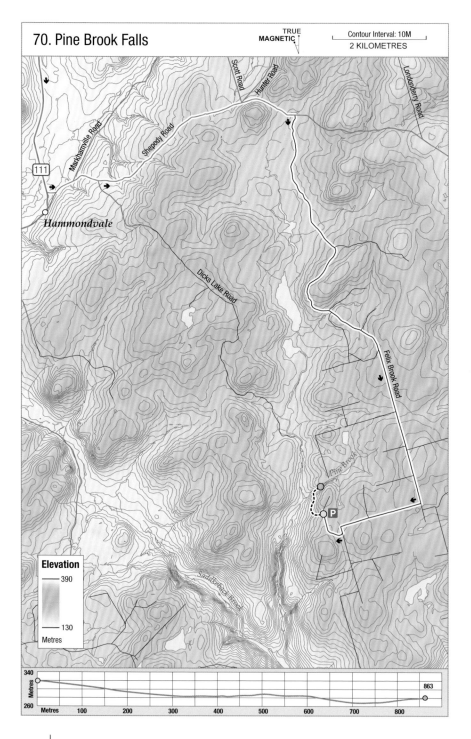

70. Pine Brook Falls

TRUE
MAGNETIC

Contour Interval: 10M
2 KILOMETRES

111

Hammondvale

Mackhamville Road

Shepody Road

Scott Road

Hunter Road

Londonderry Road

Dicks Lake Road

Felix Brook Road

Pine Brook

P

Saddleback Brook

Elevation

— 390

— 130

Metres

340
Metres
260

Metres   100   200   300   400   500   600   700   800

863

70. Pine Brook Falls

Type: Drop
Height: 5 m
Best season(s): Spring, fall
Access: Bushwhack
Source: Pine Brook
Distance (one way): 863 m
Difficulty: Moderate to difficult

Rating: 3
Hiking time: 1 hour
Land ownership: Crown
Map: NTS 021H11 Waterford
Nearby waterfall(s): Hemlock Falls
Cellphone coverage: N

Finding the trailhead: From Sussex Corner, head toward St. Martins on Route 111 and drive roughly 16 km to Hammondvale. Turn left on Shepody Road at 45°34'25.5" N, 65°30'08.3" W. Follow this road for approximately 6.5 km to 45°35'16.9" N, 65°26'02.1" W. Turn right at what is locally known as Felix Brook Road and drive approximately 10.5 km to coordinates 45°30'48.1" N, 65°24'03.2" W. Turn right and continue along the road to coordinates 45°30'28.1" N, 65°25'21.1" W. Turn right again and drive to the trailhead coordinates.

Trailhead: 45°30'41.9" N, 65°25'39.4" W   **Waterfall:** 45°30'60.0" N, 65°25'44.2" W

The hike: From the trailhead, begin a thirty-minute bushwhack to the waterfalls. This route follows the contour lines along Falls Brook to Pine Brook in order to navigate around the heavy, thick growth associated with clearcuts. The banks of the brooks have not been lumbered, leaving a gracious forest canopy that makes the hike enjoyable. It is full of the natural sounds and smells of the forest without the exposed heat of a clearcut.

With its source in the small lakes and wetlands further up the plateau, Pine Brook cuts through the craggy terrain to join with Falls Brook and, eventually, the Bay of Fundy. The brook, like many others, was used to float timber down to sawmills located near the estuary of the Big Salmon River. During the winter, lumbermen piled the trees they cut along the streambeds and on the riverbanks so the logs could be driven downriver on the spring freshet to a holding pond above the mill.

71. Hells Kitchen Falls

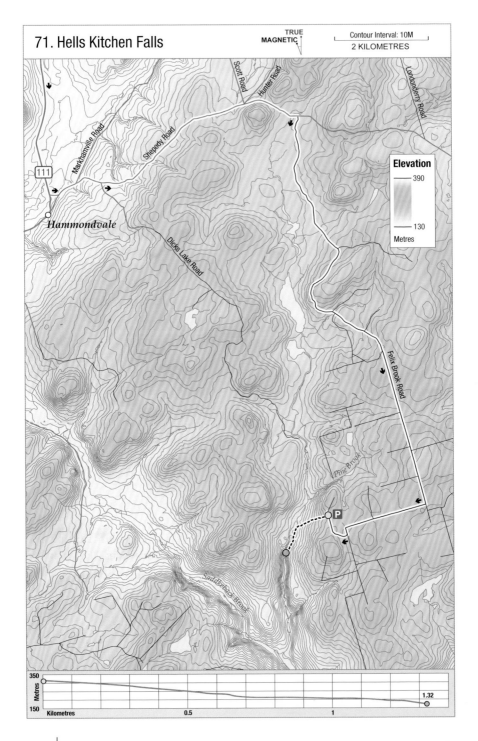

TRUE
MAGNETIC

Contour Interval: 10M
2 KILOMETRES

Scott Road
Hunter Road
Londonderry Road
Markhamville Road
Shepody Road
111
Hammondvale
Dicks Lake Road
Felix Brook Road
Pine Brook
Saddleback Brook
P

Elevation
— 390
— 130
Metres

350
Metres
150
Kilometres
0.5
1
1.32

71. Hells Kitchen Falls

Type: Tiered
Height: 10 m
Best season(s): Spring, summer, fall
Access: Bushwhack
Source: Falls Brook
Distance (one way): 1.32 km
Difficulty: Moderate to difficult

Rating: 5
Hiking time: 1 hour
Land ownership: Crown
Map: NTS 021H11 Waterford
Nearby waterfall(s): Pine Brook Falls, Hemlock Brook Falls
Cellphone coverage: N

Finding the trailhead: From Sussex Corner, head towards St. Martins on Route 111 and drive roughly 16 km to Hammondvale. Turn left on Shepody Road at 45°34'25.5" N, 65°30'08.3" W and drive approximately 6.5 km to 45°35'16.9" N, 65°26'02.1" W. Turn right at what is commonly known as Felix Brook Road and drive approximately 10.5 km to coordinates 45°30'48.1" N, 65°24'03.2" W. Turn right, and continue along this road to coordinates 45°30'28.1" N, 65°25'21.1" W. Turn right once again, and drive out to the trailhead coordinates.

Trailhead: 45°30'41.9" N, 65°25'39.4" W   **Waterfall:** 45°30'17.1" N, 65°26'21.2" W

The hike: Also known as Little Dam Falls, this waterfall's natural ambience and rugged terrain make it a stunning location to photograph. The bushwhack leads down through an old-growth forest over a blanket of moss to the edge of Falls Brook. For the most part, the forest is open, making the hike manageable. Continue downstream, following the brook's relentless churn. It is a rough watercourse, and in no time, the first series of waterfalls can be heard.

Continue further downstream to the second set. All the while, the ravine is narrowing, and the terrain is becoming wilder. The last in the series of falls is Hells Kitchen, a spectacular double-tiered falls, located in a narrow notch. Because of its orientation, the whole series of falls is very difficult to photograph unless you hike down below the waterfall to a clearing for an unobstructed view. Combining this waterfall with the nearby Pine Brook Falls and Hemlock Brook Falls makes for an excellent day.

72. Hemlock Brook Falls

Type: Drop
Height: 12 m
Best season(s): Spring, fall
Access: Trail, bushwhack
Source: Hemlock Brook
Distance (one way): 1.3 km
Difficulty: Moderate to difficult

Rating: 4
Hiking time: 1.5 hours
Land ownership: Crown
Map: NTS 021H11 Waterford
Nearby waterfall(s): Pine Brook Falls, Hell's Kitchen Falls
Cellphone coverage: N

Finding the trailhead: From Sussex Corner, head toward St. Martins on Route 111 and drive roughly 16 km to Hammondvale. Turn left on Shepody Road at 45°34'25.5" N, 65°30'08.3" W and drive for approximately 6.5 km to 45°35'16.9" N, 65°26'02.1" W. Turn right onto what is commonly known as Felix Brook Road and drive approximately 10.5 km to coordinates 45°30'48.1" N, 65°24'03.2" W. Turn right on this road and continue for 3 km before turning right onto the road at 45°30'03.2" N, 65°25'11.8" W and driving downhill roughly 700 m. This road starts off with promise but narrows toward the end with little space to turn a vehicle, so parking here is suggested.

72. Hemlock Brook Falls

TRUE
MAGNETIC

Contour Interval: 10M
2 KILOMETRES

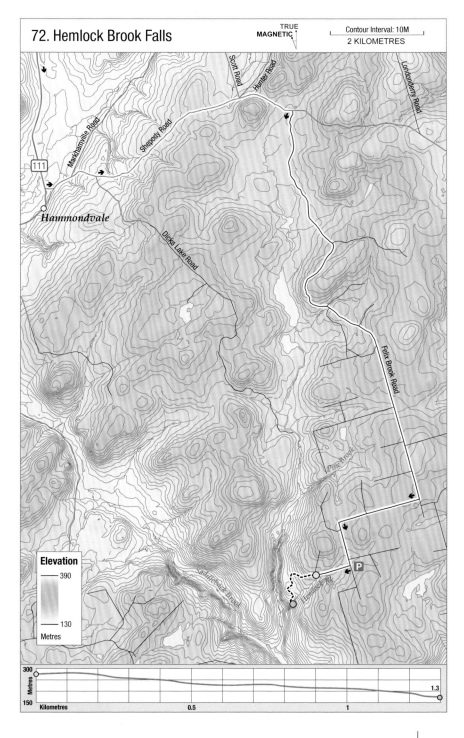

Scott Road

Hunter Road

Londonderry Road

Markhamville Road

Shepody Road

111

Hammondvale

Dicks Lake Road

Felix Brook Road

Pine Brook

P

Elevation

— 390

— 130
Metres

Saddleback Brook

Hemlock Rd

Trailhead: 45°29'57.1" N, 65°25'47.0" W
Waterfall: 45°29'39.1" N, 65°26'08.7" W

The hike: Hemlock Brook trundles through the steep valley formed by Falls Brook in the eastern reaches of Saint John County. Hike down the woods road, heading for the waterfall coordinates. The trail turns right and arcs back to eventually end in a clearing. This area is used by folks fishing or hunting in the valley. Cross the clearing and hike along the trail, which eventually swings right with a bushwhack down to a semblance of a trail along the brook.

There are two waterfalls of note. The first is a tiered fall with two levels, separated by a deep, dark punchbowl. About 40 m downstream, there is a second waterfall worth mentioning. It is a drop falls, sheltered within vertical cliff walls reaching 30 m skyward.

72. Hemlock Brook Falls

73. Bonnell Brook Falls

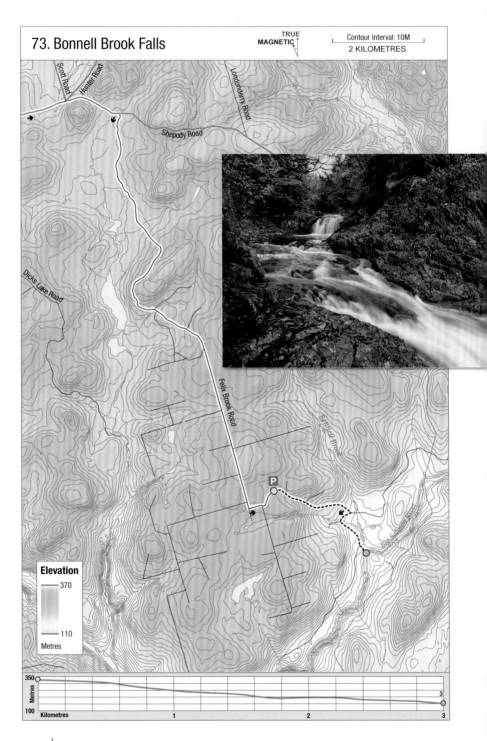

Scott Road
Hunter Road
Londonderry Road
Shepody Road
Dicks Lake Road
Felix Brook Road
Bonnell Brook
P

Elevation
370
110
Metres

350
Metres
100
Kilometres   1   2   3   3

73. Bonnell Brook Falls

Type: Tiered
Height: 9 m
Best season(s): Spring, summer, fall
Access: Trail, bushwhack
Source: Bonnell Brook
Distance (one way): 3 km
Difficulty: Moderate to difficult

Rating: 3
Hiking time: 2 hours
Land ownership: Crown
Map: NTS 021H11 Waterford
Nearby waterfall(s): Hemlock Brook Falls
Cellphone coverage: N

Finding the trailhead: From Sussex Corner, head toward St. Martins on Route 111 and drive roughly 16 km to Hammondvale. Turn left on Shepody Road at 45°34'25.5" N, 65°30'08.3" W and continue for approximately 6.5 km to 45°35'16.9" N, 65°26'02.1" W. Turn right onto what is commonly known as Felix Brook Road and drive approximately 10.7 km to coordinates 45°30'44.0" N, 65°24'01.3" W. Turn left and then left again at 45°30'45.7" N, 65°23'48.3" W. Drive to the trailhead and park; driving beyond this point requires an ATV.

Trailhead: 45°30'56.1" N, 65°23'36.1" W **Waterfall:** 45°30'13.7" N, 65°22'08.8" W

The hike: Begin hiking along the boulder-strewn road until the T junction at 45°30'40.2" N, 65°22'21.3" W. Turn right and head south, crossing a brook, to 45°30'17.4" N, 65°22'14.0" W where a short bushwhack from the trail to the waterfall is required. Head through the woods toward the brook and then continue further downstream to the waterfalls. A tributary of the Big Salmon River, Bonnell Brook drains a series of small lakes and wetlands in the Southern New Brunswick Uplands ecoregion. This area has been extensively clearcut in the last thirty years, making water levels unpredictable after heavy rains, especially during the spring freshet.

The stunning Bonnell Brook Falls is situated in a secluded twisting ravine at the confluence with the Big Salmon River. There are two waterfalls that are 15 m apart. The first drops 3 m and the second a further 6 m. We took time here to breathe in the beautiful fresh air and enjoy the natural, serene setting.

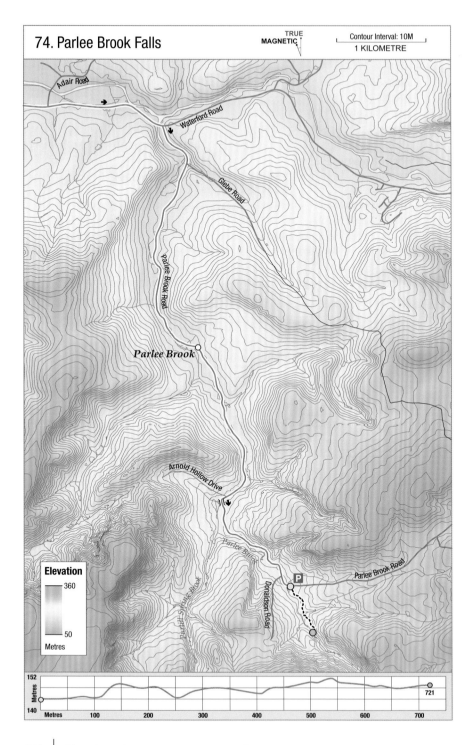

74. Parlee Brook Falls

TRUE
MAGNETIC

Contour Interval: 10M
1 KILOMETRE

Adair Road

Waterford Road

Glebe Road

Parlee Brook Road

Parlee Brook

Arnold Hollow Drive

Parlee Brook

Parlee Brook Road

Donaldson Road

Pollett-Shrunk Brook

Elevation

— 360

— 50

Metres

152

Metres

140

| Metres | 100 | 200 | 300 | 400 | 500 | 600 | 700 |

721

74. Parlee Brook Falls

Type: Drop
Height: 4 m
Best season(s): Spring, fall
Access: Bushwhack, river walk
Source: Parlee Brook
Distance (one way): 721 m
Difficulty: Moderate

Rating: 3
Hiking time: 1 hour
Land ownership: Crown
Map: NTS 021H11 Waterford
Nearby waterfall(s): Sproul Settlement
Falls
Cellphone coverage: N

Finding the trailhead: From Sussex Corner, head out on Waterford Road. Drive for approximately 6 km looking for Parlee Brook Road on the right. Follow the road up through the notch in the hills for roughly 4.5 km. Where the road splits into two roads, take the road on the left, cross the bridge, and drive 1.5 km. At this location, the road divides into Donaldson Road on the right and Parlee Brook Road on the left. Park here at the trailhead.

Trailhead: 45°38'32.6" N, 65°23'56.9" W   **Waterfall:** 45°38'16.2" N, 65°23'44.8" W

The hike: This is bushwhacking and rock-hopping at its finest, but the reward of the waterfall and pool below for swimming is worth the effort. It is one of the many falls I wanted to photograph for years and finally made time for this year with my son. Follow the sketchy trail on the east side of the brook as it extends upstream between the two roads. Within 100 m, the trail starts to diminish. Continue bushwhacking along the brook until reaching the first falls. There is a smaller second waterfall another 50 m up the brook. Parlee Brook Falls is not high, but nonetheless, it is a great location for nature lovers

and hardcore waterfall junkies to enjoy.

Bonus feature(s): On the drive back, stop at the junction of Parlee Brook Road and Arnold Hollow Drive. Hike up the hill to see both the Friars Nose rock formation at 45°38'55.1" N, 65°25'03.7" W and the Parlee Brook natural amphitheatre at 45°38'36.3" N, 65°25'47.2" W.

75. Long Beach Brook Falls

Type: Slide
Height: 4 m
Best season(s): Spring, fall
Access: Trail
Source: Long Beach Brook
Distance (one way): 779 m
Difficulty: Easy to moderate

Rating: 2
Hiking time: 20 minutes
Land ownership: Crown (Fundy Trail, fees apply)
Map: NTS 021H06 Salmon River
Nearby waterfall(s): Walton Glen Brook Falls
Cellphone coverage: Y

Finding the trailhead: The Fundy Trail Parkway main gate is located approximately 10 km east of the village of St. Martins. After paying admission, take this very picturesque parkway to Long Beach and park at P13. The trailhead is on the upper side of the road, 100 m from the parking area.

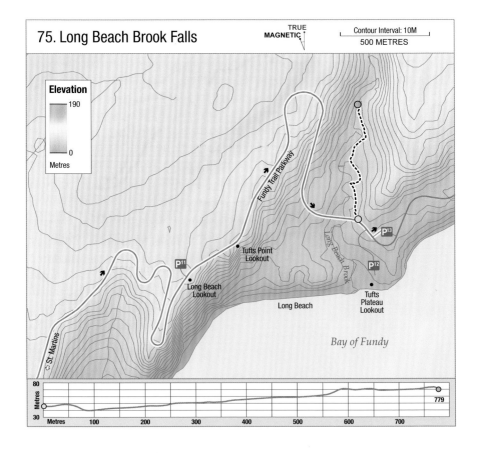

Trailhead: 45°25'48.2" N, 65°22'23.8" W   **Waterfall:** 45°26'09.0" N, 65°22'23.2" W

The hike: The falls are one of many sites to visit along the Fundy Trail Parkway. From the trailhead, follow the moderately easy footpath as it ascends away from the coast. The trail leads through open woods, is marked with a blue blaze, and has ropes in areas where some may have difficulty. The Bay of Fundy influences life along its shoreline and in the lofty hills that rise up from the bay. With its proximity to the water, the dense old-growth forest captures the cool air far up the mountainside, as is evident by the chilly temperatures at Long Beach Brook Falls. This brook and waterfall are delightful, with cool mountain water cascading throughout the ravine in a soothing rhythm, captivating visitors with its melody.

Lumbering was very important to the survival of the many small communities scattered along this coast, and Long Beach was no exception. Part of its attraction is the timeworn water turbine at the base of the falls, as well as a chain near the falls. Scattered in the woods along the path are other remnants of the old sawmill. Take time to explore our connection to the past.

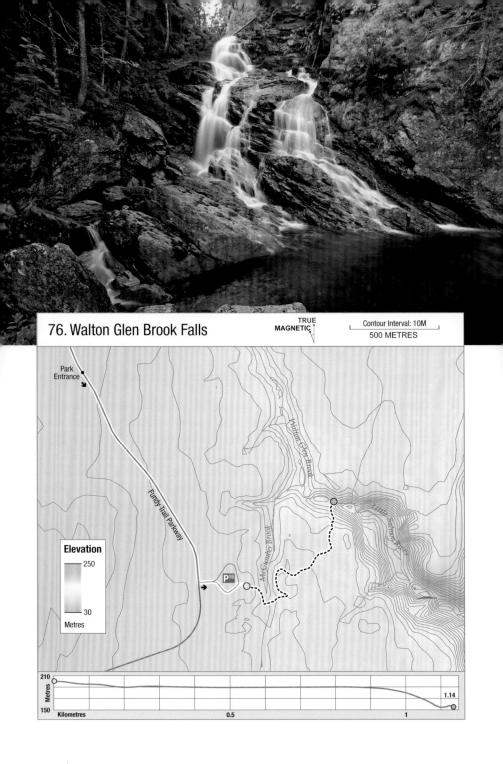

76. Walton Glen Brook Falls

TRUE
MAGNETIC

Contour Interval: 10M
500 METRES

Park
Entrance

Fundy Trail Parkway

Walton Glen Brook

McGunkey Brook

Little Salmon River

Elevation

250

30

Metres

P15

210

Metres

150

Kilometres

0.5

1

1.14

76. Walton Glen Brook Falls

Type: Tiered
Height: 35 m
Best season(s): Spring, summer, fall
Access: Trail
Source: Walton Glen Brook
Distance (one way): 1.14 km
Difficulty: Moderate to difficult

Rating: 4
Hiking time: 1 hour
Land ownership: Crown (Fundy Trail, fees apply)
Map: NTS 021H06 Salmon River
Nearby waterfall(s): Wallace Falls, Long Beach Brook Falls
Cellphone coverage: N

Finding the trailhead: From Sussex Corner, take Waterford Road through the beautiful rolling hills of Dutch Valley and Waterford. Drive roughly 12 km to the Y junction, leading to Walker Settlement Road on the right and Creek Road on the left. Follow Creek Road into the Caledonia Highlands, passing Walton Lake and a wilderness lodge, to the Fundy Trail Parkway. Continue on the parkway and pay at the entrance. Just beyond is the designated parking area for Walton Glen Gorge (P15). The trailhead is to the right of the service buildings. The trail to the gorge lookout is an easy hike.

Trailhead: 45°29'26.0" N, 65°18'30.0" W **Waterfall:** 45°29'41.0" N, 65°18'07.8" W

The hike: From the parking area, follow the pathway leading to the lookout. Just before, there is a narrow trail that zigzags down into the gorge and Walton Glen Brook Falls. This is not to be confused with the seasonal waterfall (Walton Glen Gorge Falls) that flows over the eastern edge of the gorge. An alternative is to hike to the viewing platform overlooking the Walton Glen Gorge and Falls. This waterfall is definitely seasonal, and early springtime is the best opportunity for viewing it.

Collecting waters from smaller brooks and several lesser streams further up the gorge, Walton Glen Brook is the primary brook in this magnificent gorge. Surrounded by towering cliffs and draped with trees hanging precariously, the brook cascades over three major drops that total 35 m. While down in the gorge, follow the brook over the large boulders to the Eye of the Needle, where the water has cut a channel through the bedrock. Beyond this, Walton Glen Brook rushes into the Little Salmon River on its journey to the Bay of Fundy.

Bonus fall(s): While here, hike to McLeod Brook Falls at 45°29'55.2" N, 65°18'20.5" W, named after long-time local woodsman Bentley McLeod.

77. Wallace Falls

TRUE
MAGNETIC

Contour Interval: 10M
2 KILOMETRES

Elevation
— 340

— 200
Metres

Goose Creek Road

Creek Road

Crawford Lake

Shepody Road

Fundy Trail Parkway

Grassy Lake

gravel road

P

Martin Head Overlook

Dustin Brook Road

Quiddy River

247
Metres
232

Metres   50   100   150   200   250

266

77. Wallace Falls

Type: Drop
Height: 6 m
Best season(s): Spring, summer, fall
Access: Trail
Source: Quiddy River
Distance (one way): 266 m
Difficulty: Easy to moderate

Rating: 3
Hiking time: 20 minutes
Land ownership: Crown
Map: NTS 021H11 Waterford
Nearby waterfall(s): Goose Creek Falls, Walton Glen Brook Falls
Cellphone coverage: N

Finding the trailhead: From Sussex Corner, take Waterford Road through the beautiful rolling hills of Dutch Valley and Waterford. Drive roughly 12 km to the Y junction, leading to Walker Settlement Road on the right and Creek Road on the left. Follow Creek Road into the Caledonia Highlands, passing Walton Lake and a wilderness lodge, to the Fundy Trail Parkway. On the parkway, look for the makeshift sign for Wallace (Quiddy) Falls at coordinates 45°33'53.8" N, 65°17'18.5" W. Turn left and take the gravel road for roughly 1.6 km to the access road leading to Wallace Falls at 45°33'51.4" N, 65°16'08.4" W. The trailhead is 2.9 km further, just before the ATV bridge over the Quiddy River. **Note:** As a result of the Fundy Trail Parkway extension, roads in this area are currently being rerouted and renamed. Readers are advised to use caution with online maps for this area as they have been slow to catch up to the changes. These directions and maps are correct as of summer 2020 — readers are advised to check current conditions before setting out.

Trailhead: 45°34'02.7" N, 65°13'59.7" W **Waterfall:** 45°33'55.4" N, 65°13'59.0" W

The hike: Named after early homesteaders, Wallace Falls is the most widely known of the several waterfalls on the river. The circuitous but safe trail on the west side of the Quiddy River leads to the pool at the bottom of the larger falls. Further upstream, the upper falls slide over a rock face before plunging a second time over a sheer escarpment. Adventurers may wish to take the day to explore the Quiddy River from Wallace Falls to Martin Head at the estuary. Some spots require climbing up through the mossy forests to find the next passable ravine. The best time to hike this river is during the summer since some areas are inaccessible in spring.

Bonus fall(s): There are at least six more waterfalls further downstream with two of note at 45°33'23.1" N, 65°14'03.0" W and 45°32'55.7" N, 65°13'38.2" W.

78. Tweedledum and Tweedledee Falls

Type: Tiered
Height: 12 m
Best season(s): Spring, fall
Access: Trail, shore walk, bushwhack
Source: Brandy Brook
Distance (one way): 4.9 km
Difficulty: Moderate to difficult

Rating: 3
Hiking time: 3 hours
Land ownership: Crown
Map: NTS 021H11 Waterford
Nearby waterfall(s): Goose Creek
Falls, Wallace Falls
Cellphone coverage: N

Finding the trailhead: From Sussex Corner, take Waterford Road through the beautiful rolling hills of Dutch Valley and Waterford. Drive roughly 12 km to the Y junction, leading to Walker Settlement Road on the right and Creek Road on the left. Follow Creek Road into the Caledonia Highlands, passing Walton Lake and a wilderness lodge, to the Fundy Trail Parkway. On the parkway, look for the makeshift sign for Wallace (Quiddy) Falls at coordinates 45°33'53.8" N, 65°17'18.5" W. Turn left and drive out the gravel road for 6.5 km, past the turn-off for Wallace Falls, to the junction with Goose Creek Road at 45°36'09.5" N, 65°14'08.1" W. Turn right onto this road and drive 9 km to Martin Head, passing

TRUE
MAGNETIC

Contour Interval: 10M

3 KILOMETRES

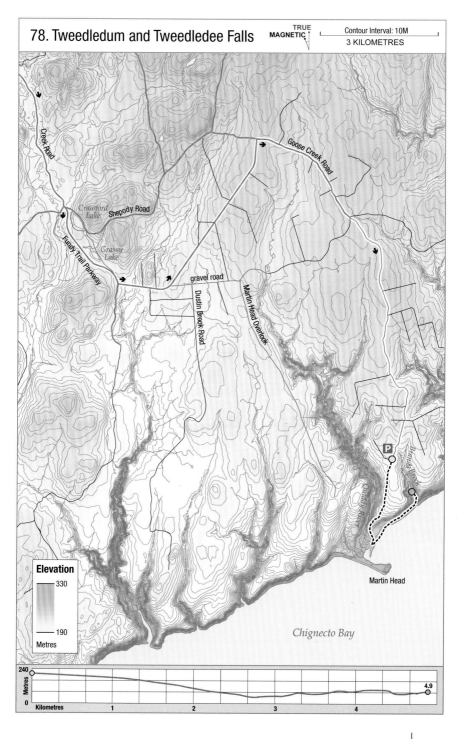

Elevation

330

190

Metres

Martin Head

Chignecto Bay

240
Metres
0
Kilometres   1   2   3   4
4.9

the trailhead to Goose Creek Falls. Park near the crest of the long hill to the beach.

The entire length of Goose Creek Road is rough, and unless the hill portion has been graded, it is not drivable without an ATV. Check the tide times before visiting these two waterfalls. **Note:** As a result of the Fundy Trail Parkway extension, roads in this area are currently being rerouted and renamed. Readers are advised to use caution with online maps for this area as they have been slow to catch up to the changes. These directions and maps are correct as of summer 2020 — readers are advised to check current conditions before setting out.

Trailhead: 45°31'05.9" N, 65°11'08.6" W
Waterfall: 45°30'32.5" N, 65°10'42.9" W

The hike: Hike 2.8 km down the road to the beach and turn east along the rugged shore to Brandy Brook. There is a "rock garden" to navigate before heading inland and up the brook to Tweedledum and Tweedledee Falls. The water in the brook is clear and the colour of brandy or gin, depending on the light. If the tide begins to return and cuts off the beach route, use the Fundy Footpath to return to Goose Creek Road. This roundabout route is rather long, but the vistas and beach at Martin Head are beautiful, as well as the large "boulder garden" near the mouth of the brook. It is a supernatural location on an amazing bay.

78. Tweedledum and Tweedledee Falls

79. Goose Creek Falls

TRUE
MAGNETIC

Contour Interval: 10M

3 KILOMETRES

Elevation

330

190

Metres

Creek Road

Goose Creek Road

Crawford Lake

Shepody Road

Fundy Trail Parkway

Grassy Lake

gravel road

Dustin Brook Road

Martin Head Overlook

P

320

Metres

200

Kilometres

0.5

1

1.5

1.6

79. Goose Creek Falls

Type: Drop
Height: 12 m
Best season(s): Summer, fall
Access: Bushwhack, river walk
Source: Goose Creek (Saint John)
Distance (one way): 1.6 km
Difficulty: Moderate to difficult

Rating: 4
Hiking time: 1 hour
Land ownership: Crown
Map: NTS 021H11 Waterford
Nearby waterfall(s): Wallace Falls
Cellphone coverage: N

Finding the trailhead: From Sussex Corner, take Waterford Road through the beautiful rolling hills of Dutch Valley and Waterford. Drive roughly 12 km to the Y junction, leading to Walker Settlement Road on the right and Creek Road on the left. Follow Creek Road into the Caledonia Highlands, passing Walton Lake and a wilderness lodge, to the Fundy Trail Parkway. On the parkway, look for the makeshift sign for Wallace (Quiddy) Falls at coordinates 45°33'53.8" N, 65°17'18.5" W. Turn left onto a gravel road, drive 6.5 km past the turnoff for Wallace Falls to 45°36'09.5" N, 65°14'08.1" W, and turn right onto Goose Creek Road, also known as Martin Head Overlook Road. Drive roughly 6.5 km on this rough road to the trailhead.

Note: As a result of the Fundy Trail Parkway extension, roads in this area are currently being rerouted and renamed. Readers are advised to use caution with online maps for this area as they have been slow to catch up to the changes. These directions and maps are correct as of summer 2020 — readers are advised to check current conditions before setting out.

Trailhead: 45°33'44.5" N, 65°11'20.1" W   **Waterfall:** 45°34'03.9" N, 65°10'24.7" W

The hike: From the trailhead, hike the grown-in road roughly 1.2 km to the end and bushwhack down a gentle slope to the creek. Head upstream to the highest of several waterfalls. There are bonus waterfalls upstream and downstream, where the sheer cliffs are worn to bare rock. Goose Creek starts in the marshy bogs located in the Caledonia Highlands plateau. Black spruce and larch thrive in the thick carpet of sphagnum moss, and the bogs and streams support many animals, in particular moose and beaver. Similar to other waterways in the Fundy region, Goose Creek has carved a deep ravine through the bedrock, producing a roguish watercourse with an outstanding diversity of flora and geological features.

Bonus fall(s): Three extremely beautiful waterfalls to tackle are at the following coordinates: 45°34'21.0" N, 65°10'43.0" W; 45°33'44.4" N, 65°09'55.3" W; and 45°33'12.8" N, 65°09'40.4" W.

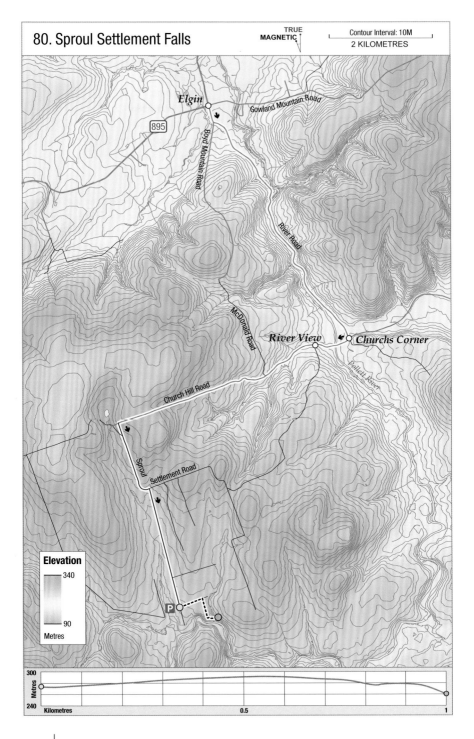

80. Sproul Settlement Falls

TRUE
MAGNETIC

Contour Interval: 10M

2 KILOMETRES

Elgin

Gowland Mountain Road

895

Boyd Mountain Road

River Road

McDonald Road

River View

Churchs Corner

Pollett River

Church Hill Road

Sproul Settlement Road

Elevation

340

90

Metres

P

300

Metres

240

Kilometres

0.5

1

80. Sproul Settlement Falls

Type: Tiered
Height: 14 m
Best season(s): Spring, fall
Access: Bushwhack, trail
Source: Unidentified
Distance (one way): 1 km
Difficulty: Moderate to difficult

Rating: 4
Hiking time: 30 minutes
Land ownership: Crown
Map: NTS 021H11 Waterford
Nearby waterfall(s): Pollett River Falls
Cellphone coverage: N

Finding the trailhead: From the community of Elgin, drive out River Road to Churchs Corner, following the beautiful Pollett River. At the four corners, turn right and drive west 5.6 km on Church Hill Road. At coordinates 45°44'34.0" N, 65°07'59.3" W, turn left on Sproul Settlement Road and drive 1.5 km to 45°43'53.4" N, 65 07'33.2" W. Turn right and drive the rough gravel road approximately 2.3 km to the trailhead to park.

Trailhead: 45°42'39.7" N, 65°07'08.3" W
Waterfall: 45°42'32.5" N, 65°06'37.6" W

The hike: Push through the brush on an overgrown woods road on the left for roughly 450 m until reaching an ATV trail on the right. Hike down it about 375 m and take the pathway to a rocky outcrop where there are excellent views of the top of the falls. Sproul Settlement Falls plunges and then cascades over bedrock, forming a double-tiered waterfall before emptying into the Pollett River. The trail eventually leads to the base of the waterfall. The best way to fully appreciate it is from the bottom, but be careful; the trail is steep leading to the stream and the apex of the waterfall. Be aware of footing on the moisture-laden rocks.

The community of Sproul Settlement, named after the eponymous family who settled there, is long gone, taken back by nature. All that remains is the waterfall that was there before the settlers arrived and will be there long after our departure. It is difficult to fathom that a small settlement once existed here. The name is an epitaph to the determination of the early settlers.

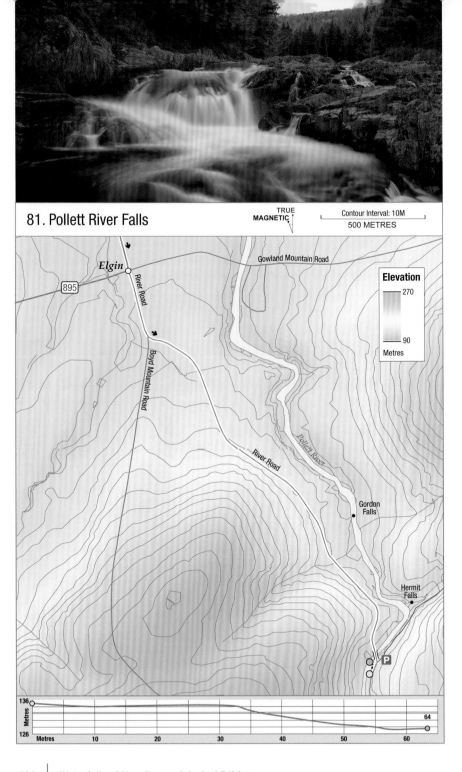

81. Pollett River Falls

TRUE
MAGNETIC

Contour Interval: 10M
500 METRES

Gowland Mountain Road

Elgin

895

River Road

Boyd Mountain Road

River Road

Pollett River

Elevation

270

90

Metres

Gordon
Falls

Hermit
Falls

P

136

Metres

64

126

Metres   10   20   30   40   50   60

81. Pollett River Falls

Type: Cascade
Height: 5 m
Best season(s): Year-round
Access: Trail
Source: Pollett River
Distance (one way): 64 m
Difficulty: Moderate

Rating: 2
Hiking time: 5 minutes
Land ownership: Crown
Map: NTS 021H14 Petitcodiac
Nearby waterfall(s): Sproul Falls
Cellphone coverage: Y

Finding the trailhead: Drive to Petitcodiac and take Route 905 south toward the rural hamlet of Elgin. In Elgin, the transition between the New Brunswick Lowlands and the Caledonia Highlands is very obvious. The road meanders roughly 17 km through lush forest before emerging into an expansive valley. Continue through Elgin until the Y junction and stay left on River Road to the bridge crossing the Pollett River. Park here — but do not block the road — and cross to the trailhead.

Trailhead: 45°46'48.5" N, 65°05'40.6" W **Waterfall:** 45°46'50.2" N, 65°05'40.4" W

The hike: Climb over the guardrail on the upriver side of the bridge and follow the trail down along the roadside and bridge. The Pollett River carves a torturous route from the Caledonia Highlands down through a precipitous valley covered with mixed conifer and deciduous forest. The largest tributary in the Petitcodiac River watershed, it forms steep ravines and waterfalls on its way to the Petitcodiac River. The granite geology at Pollett River Falls contrasts with the conglomerate formations a few kilometres downriver at Gordon Falls.

Bonus fall(s): From the parking area, hike up the gravel road to the trail leading to Gibson Brook and Hermit Falls at 45°46'57.1" N, 65°05'32.1" W. This brook rushes down from Gowland Mountain through an extremely narrow and cavernous ravine to meet the Pollett River at one of the most incredible river gorges in New Brunswick. The second bonus falls is Gordon Falls, located further down the Pollett River at 45°47'11.3" N, 65°05'46.3" W. The best time to photograph these waterfalls is on an overcast day in autumn.

82. East Branch Point Wolfe River Falls

Type: Cascade
Height: 4 m
Best season(s): Summer, fall
Access: Trail, bushwhack
Source: East Branch Point Wolfe River
Distance (one way): 1.4 km
Difficulty: Moderate to extreme

Rating: 4
Hiking time: 90 minutes
Land ownership: Crown
Map: NTS 021H11 Waterford
Nearby waterfall(s): Haley Brook Falls
Cellphone coverage: N

Finding the trailhead: Take Route 1 east to the Penobsquis exit for Fundy National Park on Route 114. Just before the park entrance, turn right onto the newly upgraded Shepody Road. Drive roughly 2 km to the access road and turn left at 45°39'21.5" N, 65°10'32.5" W. Head south on this road for roughly

82. East Branch Point Wolfe River Falls

TRUE
MAGNETIC

Contour Interval: 10M
1500 METRES

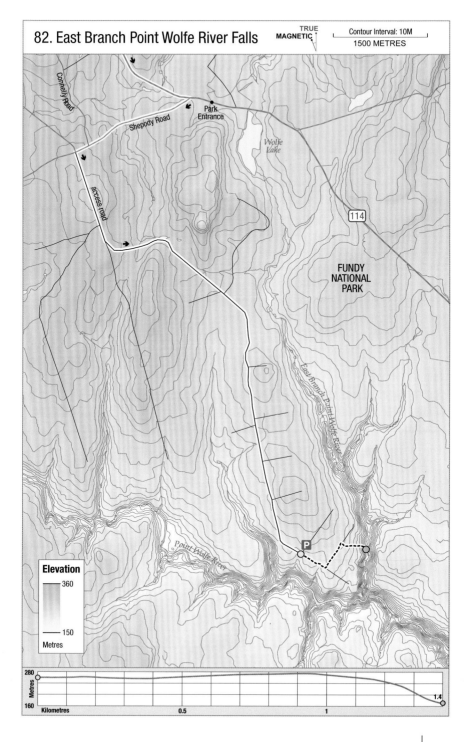

Connelly Road

Shepody Road

Park Entrance

Wolfe Lake

access road

114

FUNDY NATIONAL PARK

East Branch Point Wolfe River

P

Point Wolfe River

Elevation

360

150

Metres

280
Metres
160

Kilometres   0.5   1   1.4

1.5 km, staying to the left at the Y junction and continuing 7 km to the trailhead. Begin hiking from this point unless the road has been improved.

Trailhead: 45°35'53.0" N, 65°07'49.9" W   **Waterfall:** 45°35'56.4" N, 65°07'01.5" W

The hike: Warning!! This is an extremely difficult hike in a wilderness location. It requires a high level of physical fitness, especially in the descent and ascent from the gorge. From the parking location, the hike follows an old logging road for roughly 950 m before a bushwhack through an old-growth forest. Near the falls, a difficult descent begins with a quick drop toward the river and waterfalls. The East Branch Point Wolfe River is very much a wilderness river that forms the western boundary of Fundy National Park. With its source at Wolfe Lake, the river has ripped through the mountains to form an austere and picturesque gorge, especially near its confluence with the Point Wolfe River. Here, cliffs rise up to 61 m, making the area extremely difficult to hike.

Bonus fall(s): The two bonus waterfalls at 45°35'36.5" N, 65°07'04.4" W and 45°35'32.4" N, 65°07'03.3" W are for individuals with a sense of adventure. They require physical fitness and hiking acuity. Both are challenging!!

Bonus falls on the East
Branch Pointe Wolfe River

83. Haley Brook Falls

TRUE
MAGNETIC

Contour Interval: 10M
2 KILOMETRES

Elevation
360
220
Metres

Park Entrance
Grassy Lake
Shepody Road
Wolfe Lake
FUNDY NATIONAL PARK
114

226
Metres
218
Metres   100   200   300
341

83. Haley Brook Falls

Type: Tiered
Height: 4 m
Best season(s): Spring, fall
Access: Bushwhack
Source: Haley Brook
Distance (one way): 341 m
Difficulty: Moderate

Rating: 3
Hiking time: 20 minutes
Land ownership: Crown (Fundy National Park, fees apply)
Map: NTS 021H11 Waterford
Nearby waterfall(s): Upper Falls, Third Vault Brook
Cellphone coverage: N

Finding the trailhead: Head for Fundy National Park from the west on Route 114. Just beyond the Wolfe Lake picnic area, look for the sign for Shepody Road. Turn left and head out the gravel road approximately 9.5 km to Haley Brook and park just beyond the brook. The trailhead is on the right.

Trailhead: 45°41'27.7" N, 65°01'31.9" W   **Waterfall:** 45°41'21.7" N, 65°01'21.7" W

The hike: Begin bushwhacking down along the east side of the brook from the roadside. Unlike the trails to many of the waterfalls in the park, there is no groomed pathway. The hike is through an old-growth forest, and near the waterfalls, a thick carpet of sphagnum moss covers the forest floor, making it wet underfoot. Continue hiking to just below the falls for the finest viewing and photographing location. Unlike the upper falls at Third Vault Brook and Laverty Falls, Haley Brook Falls is one of the lesser known in Fundy National Park. The geology here is conglomerate with remnants of the Maritime Basin and is similar to the Hopewell Rocks. Over time, the watercourse has carved and smoothed the rock. Overall, it is a very pleasant location.

The historic Shepody Road, also known as Immigrant Road, forms the northern boundary of Fundy National Park. Many of the Irish immigrants that made Albert County their home travelled the long distance along this road to settle land in the Caledonia Highlands.

84. Upper Falls, Third Vault Brook

Type: Drop
Height: 20 m
Best season(s): Spring, summer, fall
Access: Trail, bushwhack, river walk
Source: Third Vault Brook
Distance (one way): 3.8 km
Difficulty: Moderate to extreme

Rating: 4
Hiking time: 2 hours
Land ownership: Crown (Fundy National Park, fees apply)
Map: NTS 021H11 Waterford
Nearby waterfall(s): Haley Brook Falls
Cellphone coverage: N

Finding the trailhead: To find the upper falls of Third Vault Brook, head for Fundy National Park from the west on Route 114. From the northern entrance to the park, drive roughly 12 km on the lookout for Laverty Road on the left. Turn here and drive approximately 1 km to the parking area on the right. The trailhead is well marked.

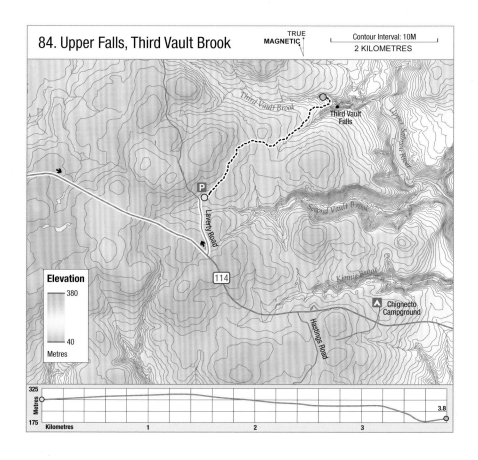

Trailhead: 45°37'29.4" N, 65°01'32.8" W
Waterfall: 45°38'29.6" N, 64°59'45.9" W

The hike: From the trailhead, follow the park trail for roughly 3.4 km, eventually coming to a set of stairs at the beginning of the descent to Third Vault Falls. To reach the upper falls, turn left at this point and bushwhack down through the old-growth forest to the ravine. Then begin rock-hopping upstream about 200 m to the upper falls of Third Vault Brook. Be prepared to get your boots wet and dirty.

The upper falls is the less known of the two and does not possess the striking beauty of the lower falls, but nonetheless, it attracts attention, especially during the spring freshet. The mountain ridges along the Upper Salmon River rise precipitously from the ravine, providing the area with a serene sense of remoteness. There is no natural amphitheater here, but a cluster of large boulders holds small pools of water at the base of the waterfall. Large hardwood and softwood trees maintain the moist air, giving the small ravine a fragrant forest aroma. It is a waterfall that allows the visitor to get close and watch as the brook catapults over the edge of the ravine.

Bonus fall(s): Third Vault Falls is only a stone's throw away downriver at 45°38'24.3" N, 64°59'35.2" W. Hike back to the main trail and continue several hundred metres as the trail leads further down into the ravine. While on this hike, take time to photograph the smaller moss-covered cascade on the secondary brook that flows into the ravine.

Third Vault Falls (bonus falls)

85. Beaver Brook Falls

TRUE
MAGNETIC

Contour Interval: 10M
1 KILOMETRE

access road

New Ireland Road

Beaver Brook

Trout Brook

Crooks Brook

114

Elevation
360

10
Metres

P

260
Metres
160

Metres   100   200   300   400   500   600   700   800
803

85. Beaver Brook Falls

Type: Fan
Height: 25 m
Best season(s): Spring, fall
Access: Trail, bushwhack
Source: Beaver Brook
Distance (one way): 803 m
Difficulty: Moderate to difficult

Rating: 4
Hiking time: 40 minutes
Land ownership: Crown
Map: NTS 021H10 Alma
Nearby waterfall(s): Bough Brook Falls
Cellphone coverage: N

Finding the trailhead: From Route 114 between Riverside-Albert and Alma, turn right at 45°43'56.9" N, 64°45'16.1" W onto New Ireland Road and drive roughly 6 km to 45°45'00.8" N, 64°48'57.0" W. Turn left onto the access road and head south for about 2.4 km to the trailhead and park.

Trailhead: 45°43'57.5" N, 64°48'09.5" W **Waterfall:** 45°44'06.1" N, 64°48'37.4" W

The hike: Hike west to the valley's edge on the lookout for an old logging road on the right. Follow the old road as it descends into the valley and eventually reaches Beaver Brook. At the brook, begin hiking upstream toward the falls. There is no defined path; therefore, hike along the contour of the valley, weaving through the woods toward the falls. The valley starts narrowing to form a ravine and eventually forces a scramble up and over a rock outcrop near the falls. Once around the outcrop, an impressive 25 m waterfall presents itself.

Beaver Brook has its source in the Caledonia Highlands near the divide between waters flowing northeast into Crooked Creek and flowing southwest into the Beaver Brook Marsh and Shepody River. In the fall, enthusiasts are treated to a rich tapestry of autumn colours, patterns, and textures where this valley tapers to the waterfall.

86. Bough Brook Falls

Type: Tiered
Height: 3 m
Best season(s): Spring, fall
Access: Bushwhack
Source: Bough Brook
Distance (one way): 469 m
Difficulty: Moderate

Rating: 3
Hiking time: 40 minutes
Land ownership: Crown
Map: NTS 021H10 Alma
Nearby waterfall(s): Beaver Brook
Falls
Cellphone coverage: Y

Finding the trailhead: From Route 114 between Riverside-Albert and Alma, take the gravel New Ireland Road into the Caledonia Highlands for 12.5 km until 45°43'42.1" N, 64°53'20.5" W. Turn left and drive along the access road approximately 1.8 km and turn left at 45°43'06.31" N, 64°53'39.4" W. Drive 1.3 km to 45°42'25.4" N, 64°53'21.9" W, turn left again, and continue 160 m to 45°42'26.6" N, 64°53'14.5" W. Turn right and drive approximately 800 m to a Y junction. Stay to the left and continue to the end of the access road.

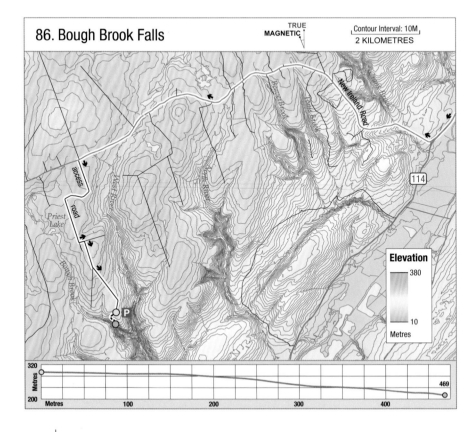

Trailhead: 45°41'18.9" N, 64°52'33.9" W **Waterfall:** 45°41'08.7" N, 64°52'36.2" W

The hike: After parking, begin bushwhacking into the woods on the right side of the road in a southwesterly direction down to the brook. From here, hike down alongside the brook (known locally as Bough Brook); this ravine must be taken seriously as it drops steeply to the brook in places. In good water conditions, there are several 2 m to 3 m waterfalls to explore and photograph.

This is hilly country with elevations of approximately 380 m, defined by narrow ravines. The brook flows in a southeasterly direction, tumbling through a narrow ravine in the plateau to the West River in an area traditionally known as New Ireland. It continues down around West River Mountain until it forms part of Germantown Marsh and, eventually, the Shepody River.

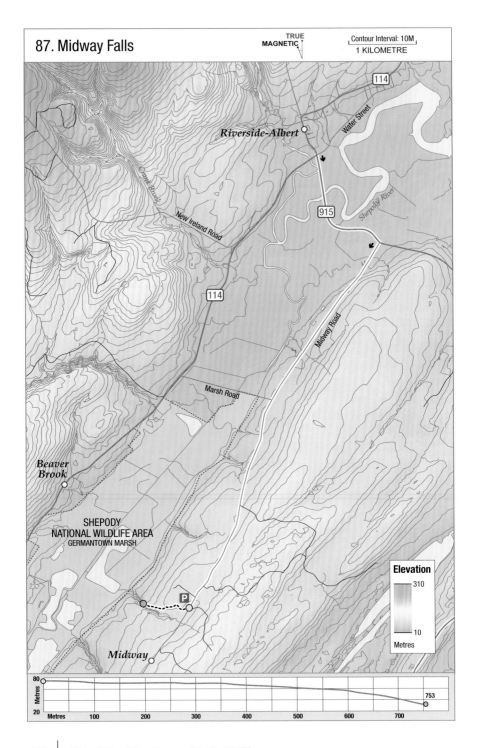

114

Riverside-Albert

Water Street

Cradle Brook

New Ireland Road

915

Shepody River

114

Midway Road

Marsh Road

Beaver Brook

SHEPODY
NATIONAL WILDLIFE AREA
GERMANTOWN MARSH

P

Elevation
310
10
Metres

Midway

Metres
80
20

Metres 100 200 300 400 500 600 700

753

87. Midway Falls

Type: Cascade
Height: 4 m
Best season(s): Spring, fall
Access: Bushwhack, river walk
Source: Unidentified
Distance (one way): 753 m
Difficulty: Moderate

Rating: 2
Hiking time: 30 minutes
Land ownership: Private
Map: NTS 021H10 Alma
Nearby waterfall(s): Beaver Brook Falls
Cellphone coverage: Y

Finding the trailhead: At the intersection in Riverside-Albert for Harvey or Alma, continue on Route 915 to Harvey. Drive roughly 1.8 km to Midway Road. Turn right onto Midway and drive west for approximately 6 km to the trailhead and park alongside the road.

Trailhead: 45°41'02.5" N, 64°45'59.7" W   **Waterfall:** 45°41'05.0" N, 64°46'30.9" W

The hike: There is no defined trailhead, so follow the ATV trail downward through an old cut and eventually into the woods. The hike follows the east side of the brook and, within minutes, the sound of the lower falls can be heard. The brook flows in a northerly direction and is a tributary of the Shepody River. Take time to explore all the waterfalls by bushwhacking up along the brook. There are remnants of old cars, along with old pots and pans discarded along the brook. The finest time to photograph the waterfalls is late September.

88. Slacks Cove Falls

Type: Cascade
Height: 3 m
Best season(s): Spring, fall
Access: Trail
Source: Unidentified
Distance (one way): 48 m
Difficulty: Easy

Rating: 2
Hiking time: 1 minute
Land ownership: Crown
Map: NTS 021H10 Alma
Nearby waterfall(s): Sea Glass Falls
Cellphone coverage: Y

Finding the trailhead: Head west out of Sackville on Route 106. On the outskirts of town, turn left onto Route 935 toward Wood Point and Rockport. Follow this paved road for roughly 20 km as it turns to gravel. Where Route 935 turns away from the shore, continue straight along Lower Rockport Road toward Lower Rockport and Cape Maringouin. Slacks Cove is approximately 6.7 km along this gravel road, with Cape Maringouin a bit further. The last section of road can be rutted and muddy unless recently graded. There is a parking area near the cairn denoting early settlers.

Trailhead: 45°43'32.9" N, 64°31'34.0" W   **Waterfall:** 45°43'31.6" N, 64°31'33.4" W

88. Slacks Cove Falls

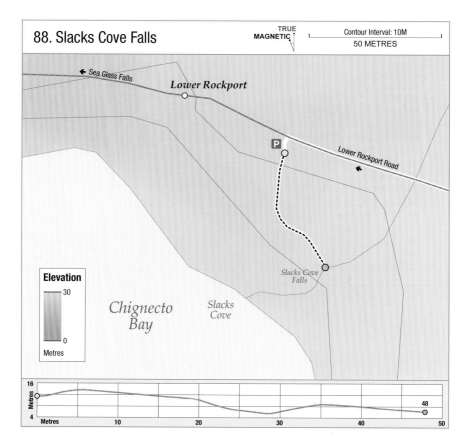

The hike: This is not a large brook or waterfall, but its redeeming features are the history and outstanding scenery. Just beyond and to the left of the cairn celebrating the early settlers from Swansea, Massachusetts, who landed near the cove in 1763, there is a well-used path leading through the woods to the falls. At the falls, there are fossils from the Carboniferous era.

The finest time to view the falls is at low tide or after a heavy rain. It is a stunning point, nearly surrounded by tidal water, with great views in practically every direction. The persistent winds have deformed and gnarled the surrounding spruce trees. While at the site, enjoy the extreme tides of the Bay of Fundy that erode the land and expose the bedrock. This is a fantastic place for observing the migration of semipalmated sandpipers and ducks, such as the American black duck, in the spring and fall.

Bonus fall(s): Sea Glass Falls is located at 45°43'36.0" N, 64°33'8.0" W. From the parking area, follow the woods trail 800 m to a clearing. Take the trail on the left to a fork in the path at 1.8 km; a side trail on the left leads to an impressive cliff.

89. Sandburn Brook Falls
90. Little Sheephouse Brook Falls
91. Mullin Stream Falls
92. Indiantown Brook Falls
93. Devils Brook Falls
94. Libbies Falls
95. Bartholomew River Falls
96. Fall Brook Falls (York)
97. Porter Brook Falls (Northumberland)
98. Chase Brook Falls
99. Midland Falls (Queens)
100. Penniac Cascade

89

91

94

93

Sunny
Corner

Miramichi

92

McGraw Brook

Renous

96

95

97

Doaktown

Boiestown

98

99

Chipman

100

Fredericton

Oromocto

Sussex

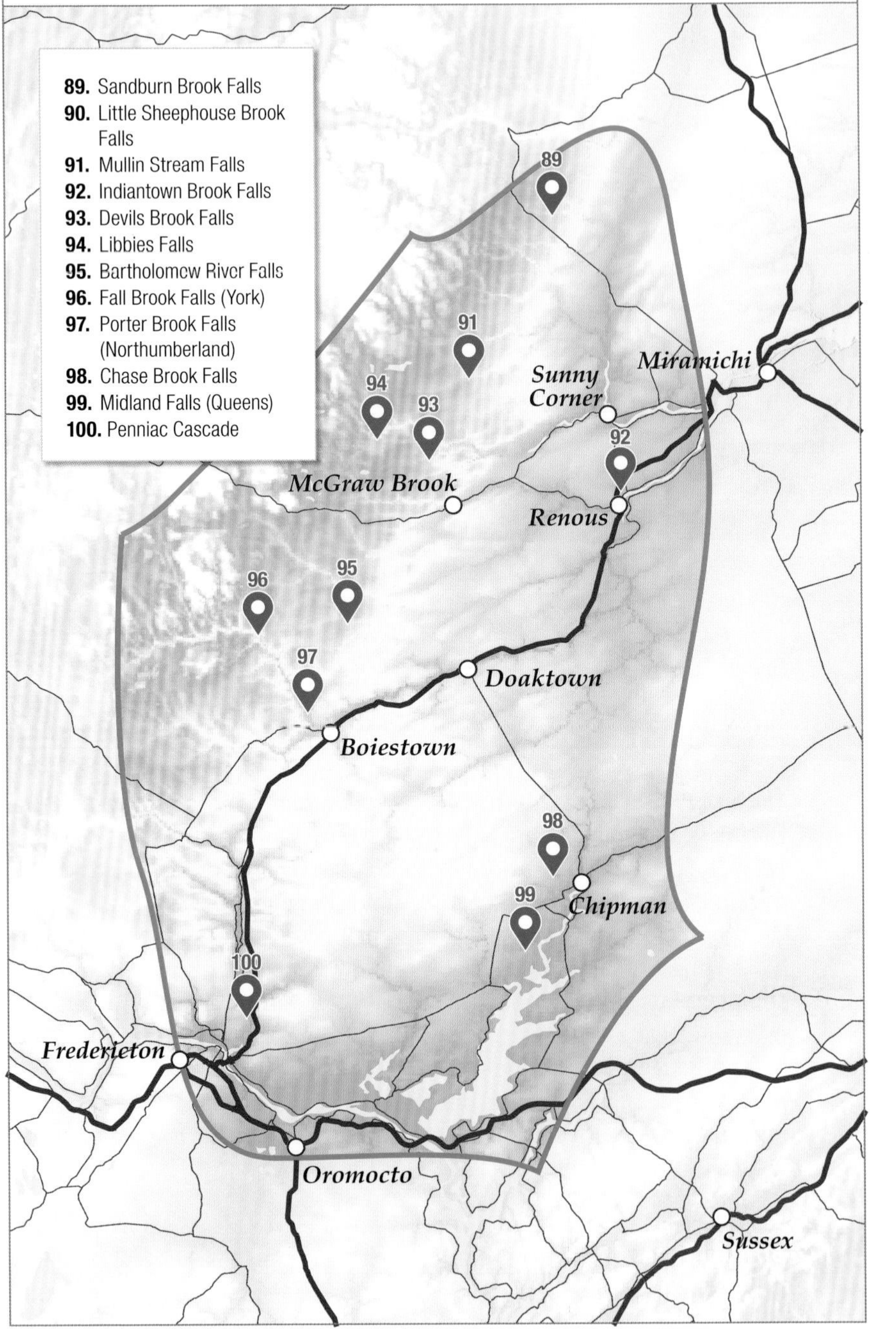

Miramichi River Route

Extending inland from the Miramichi to the provincial capital at Fredericton, this scenic route follows the length of the mighty Miramichi River to Boiestown, the geographical centre of the province. From Boiestown, the route continues along Route 8 to the Nashwaak River and further to the Wolastoq/Saint John River.

The Miramichi River is composed of numerous major tributaries and thousands of contributing streams. Its dense forests and salmon-filled waterways, contributing to what author Wayne Curtis calls the "mysticism" of the Miramichi River, have long sustained a thriving lumbering industry and an important sport fishing industry. The river is within the transition zone between the lowlands to the south and the highlands to the north. It has the majority of the waterfalls in the watershed, such as Little Sheephouse Brook Falls, Sandburn Brook Falls, and Bartholomew River Falls. The region known as the Christmas Mountains, in the timber-rich highlands of the Miramichi watershed, is a colder and wetter expanse than any other part of the province with waterways so cold that one is called the North Pole Stream. These remote streams shelter stunning waterfalls, such as Libbies Falls and Wildcat Falls, known to only a few.

As the route descends into the Nashwaak River valley, the hills diminish and the terrain begins to take on the traits of the lower Wolastoq/Saint John River valley.

92. Indiantown Brook Falls

89. Sandburn Brook Falls

TRUE
MAGNETIC

Contour Interval: 10M
1 KILOMETRE

South Branch Tomogonops River

Sandburn Brook

430

Elevation
250
160
Metres

89. Sandburn Brook Falls

Type: Tiered
Height: 3 m
Best season(s): Spring, fall
Access: Bushwhack
Source: Sandburn Brook
Distance (one way): 362 m
Difficulty: Moderate

Rating: 2
Hiking time: 20 minutes
Land ownership: Crown
Map: NTS 021P04 Sevogle
Nearby waterfall(s): Roger Brook Falls
Cellphone coverage: N

Finding the trailhead: At the junction of Route 425 and Northwest Road by the service station in Sunny Corner, drive out on Northwest Road to Wayerton on the Northwest Miramichi River. Cross the river and continue north on Route 430, locally known as Heath Steele Mines Road, to the turnoff for Sandburn Brook at 47°13'52.3" N, 65°58'38.8" W. Turn right (east) and drive out the logging road to the trailhead, a distance of 2.6 km. The area has been harvested, making the road muddy and rough in spots.

Trailhead: 47°15'00.1" N, 65°57'53.3" W **Waterfall:** 47°15'09.8" N, 65°57'57.4" W

The hike: It is a relatively short jaunt from the logging road to the falls. From the trailhead, walk north across the clearcut toward two large pine trees in the middle, roughly a distance of 200 m. Just past the first pine, turn right and walk to a third large pine tree, roughly 100 m away. At this tree, turn left and head to the end of the clearcut and into the woods to the waterfall. The sound of the brook and falls can be heard on the scramble through the woods and down into the ravine. The waterfall is located quite close to the mouth of the brook, and there is a faint trail leading to an excellent location to photograph the waterfall.

Sandburn Brook is a tributary of the South Branch Tomogonops River, which flows south to join the Northwest Miramichi River system. It's a heavily forested area and affected by harvesting practices, so expect forest debris in the brook and waterfalls. In autumn, make sure to wear hunter orange since this is a favoured hunting area and home to a large moose population.

90. Little Sheephouse Brook Falls

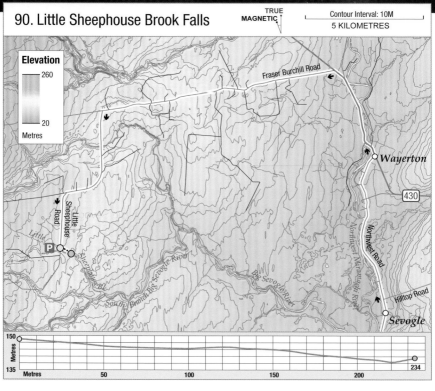

TRUE
MAGNETIC

Contour Interval: 10M
5 KILOMETRES

Elevation
260
20
Metres

Fraser Burchill Road

Little Sheephouse Road

Wayerton

430

Northwest Road

Northwest Nirthinigh River

Little Sheephouse Bk.

South Branch Big Sevogle River

Big Sevogle River

Hilltop Road

Sevogle

150
Metres
135
Metres
50
100
150
200
234

90. Little Sheephouse Brook Falls

Type: Drop
Height: 10 m
Best season(s): Spring, summer, fall
Access: Trail
Source: Little Sheephouse Brook
Distance (one way): 234 m
Difficulty: Easy

Rating: 4
Hiking time: 20 minutes
Land ownership: Crown
Map: NTS 021O01 Big Bald Mountain
Nearby waterfall(s): Sandburn Falls
Cellphone coverage: Y

Finding the trailhead: At the junction of Route 425 and Northwest Road by the service station in Sunny Corner, drive out along Northwest Road to Wayerton on the Northwest Miramichi River. Cross the river and continue to Fraser-Burchill Road at 47°09'48.9" N, 65°51'04.6" W. Turn left and follow this road for approximately 10 km then turn left onto Little Sheephouse Road. Continue for 5 km and turn left at the next sign. Follow this road approximately 2 km to the picnic area and trailhead on the left.

Trailhead: 47°05'43.9" N, 66°00'24.2" W   **Waterfall:** 47°05'40.3" N, 66°00'15.5" W

The hike: This nature park also has Hopewell Falls and Lamb Falls, but Little Sheephouse Brook Falls is considered one of the premier waterfalls in the region – if not the province. It plunges over an escarpment into a large pool, the edges garnished with mature deciduous and coniferous trees, making a natural amphitheatre. This is an excellent location for an all-ages short hike to three waterfalls and a wonderful location for youngsters to learn about the importance of preserving our natural surroundings. The trail to the observation platforms is through lush forest and is a pleasant hike. There are stairs leading to the base of the main waterfall, or you can meander further down the trail to Lamb Falls. After a few days of heavy rain, it will not disappoint. The lower and more photogenic section of Lamb Falls can be seen by hiking downriver from Little Sheephouse Brook Falls. It is well worth the effort.

William Francis Ganong hiked up Little Sheephouse Brook from the South Branch Big Sevogle, but without the success of locating the waterfall. In 1907, after exploring the entire watershed, he wrote in the *Bulletin of the Natural History Society of New Brunswick*: "The Sevogle is our most perfect wilderness river, by far the largest in New Brunswick that is wholly unsettled from source to mouth."

91. Mullin Stream Falls

TRUE
MAGNETIC

Contour Interval: 10M
5 KILOMETRES

New Mullin Stream Road

Mullin Stream

Little Sevogle River

Mullin Stream Road

Northwest Road

P

Elevation
— 290

0
Metres

Back Road

420

Sunny Corner

215

Metres

190 | Kilometres | 0.5 | 1 | 1.2

91. Mullin Stream Falls

Type: Drop
Height: 4 m
Best season(s): Spring, fall
Access: Trail
Source: Mullin Stream
Distance (one way): 1.2 km
Difficulty: Moderate

Rating: 3
Hiking time: 40 minutes
Land ownership: Crown Land
Map: NTS 021O01 Big Bald Mountain
Nearby waterfall(s): Little Sheephouse Brook Falls
Cellphone coverage: Y

Finding the trailhead: In Sunny Corner, head north on Northwest Road for about 2.3 km and turn left onto Back Road. Cross over the Northwest Miramichi River bridge and drive to Mullin Stream Road on the right. Drive out this road to New Mullin Stream Road at 46°58'40.7" N, 65°50'54.6" W. Drive along this gravel road for approximately 24 km to a Y junction at 47°00'43.0" N, 66°06'15.6" W. Stay left and, after approximately 1.6 km, take the first old logging road on the left at 47°00'38.2" N, 66°07'27.9" W. Drive on this rough road for about 1 km to a trailhead on the right.

Trailhead: 47°00'17.3" N, 66°08'38.3" W **Waterfall:** 47°00'04.3" N, 66°08'38.3" W

The hike: Mullin Stream Falls is located at the confluence of Mullin Stream and North Branch Mullin Stream. The hike is roughly 1 km. The trail to the waterfall includes some challenging sections, and there are only a few locations where you can openly view the falls. This waterfall is not particularly high, but the rock formations and large pine trees make it a beautiful site to visit. Embraced by a dense mixed forest of hardwoods and softwoods, the forest floor is scattered with trilliums and other flora in season. In low water, you can walk across to the opposite side without getting too wet. Mullin Stream has a special ambience.

92. Indiantown Brook Falls

TRUE
MAGNETIC

Contour Interval: 10M
1 KILOMETRE

Elevation

60

10

Metres

Renous

92. Indiantown Brook Falls

Type: Drop
Height: 2 m
Best season(s): Spring, fall
Access: Trail, bushwhack
Source: Indiantown Brook
Distance (one way): 601 m
Difficulty: Difficult

Rating: 3
Hiking time: 30 minutes
Land ownership: Private
Map: NTS 021I13 Newcastle
Nearby waterfall(s): Little Sheephouse
Brook Falls
Cellphone coverage: Y

Finding the trailhead: The trailhead is a logging road located on the righthand side of Route 8 heading northwest to Miramichi just beyond the Renous/Quarryville exit. The stated trailhead coordinates are at the roadside, but it is possible to drive on the logging road to the edge of the clearcut.

Trailhead: 46°50'11.4" N, 65°48'5.2" W   **Waterfall:** 46°50'4.7" N, 65°47'42.2" W

The hike: You can follow the logging road for the most part, except for a 200 m section of a tough clearcut that must be navigated. As mentioned in the introduction, clearcuts are usually hard to walk through. The 100 m bushwhack descends down through a mixed forest to the waterfall and is rather steep in places but manageable. The waterfall spans the width of the brook and is quite stunning. I was told about this waterfall many years ago at a book signing function but just did not make time to visit until writing this update.

Along the left side of the brook are the remains of an old fish ladder to help salmon on the difficult return journey to their spawning grounds further upstream. Indiantown Brook has its source in several wetlands and brooks that flow southeasterly, and it enters the Southwest Miramichi River just below its confluence with a major tributary, the Renous River. This part of the Southwest Miramichi River is a coveted salmon fishing area and is not far from Metepenagiag, the Mi'kmaq First Nations Reserve located at the head of the tide on the Miramichi River.

93. Devils Brook Falls

TRUE
MAGNETIC

Contour Interval: 10M
3 KILOMETRES

Elevation

280

60

Metres

Devils Brook

P

Little Southwest Road

Little Southwest Miramichi River

108

Renous River

McGraw Brook

198

190

Metres

92

Metres   10   20   30   40   50   60   70   80   90

93. Devils Brook Falls

Type: Tiered
Height: 3 m
Best season(s): Spring, fall
Access: Trail
Source: Devils Brook
Distance (one way): 92 m
Difficulty: Easy

Rating: 2
Hiking time: 10 minutes
Land ownership: Crown
Map: NTS 021J16 McKendrick Lake
Nearby waterfall(s): Libbies Falls
Cellphone coverage: N

Finding the trailhead: From Route 8, take exit 139 for Renous. At the intersection, turn right onto the Renous Highway (Route 108) and drive west toward Plaster Rock. At 46°49'55.8" N, 66°05'59.7" W, roughly 26 km, turn right onto the woods road known locally as Little Southwest Road. Drive north a further 12 km to the trailhead on the right and park alongside the road. The trailhead is located 10 m before the distance marker.

Trailhead: 46°52'22.3" N, 66°13'37.8" W **Waterfall:** 46°52'22.7" N, 66°13'34.3" W

The hike: Hike the old logging road down along the ridge from the main road roughly 70 m and then take the path on the left to the waterfall. The total hike is 100 m. At Devils Brook Falls, two branches of the brook converge at the waterfall, forming what would be considered a "devilish" watercourse. The falls have a rather unique location, nestled between large boulders that are wrapped together by trees that are gnarled and twisted by nature, giving the area a strange appearance. The trees are scarred from ice and high water, indicating how wild this junction must be during the spring freshet.

This is big country, where every shade of green spreads like moss, and logging roads resemble veins in a leaf, crisscrossing the landscape. The vastness and beauty of the Miramichi region of New Brunswick is humbling. The Miramichi is steeped in folklore, such as tales of the Dungarvon Whooper, with stories and music conjured up during long winters in the logging camps. One can only imagine how overwhelming this area must have seemed to those working in those camps in the 1800s.

94. Libbies Falls

Type: Tiered
Height: 8 m
Best season(s): Spring, fall
Access: Trail
Source: Libbies Brook
Distance (one way): 3.3 km
Difficulty: Easy to moderate

Rating: 5
Hiking time: 1.5 hours
Land ownership: Crown
Map: NTS 021J16 McKendrick Lake
Nearby waterfall(s): Devils Brook Falls
Cellphone coverage: N

Finding the trailhead: From Route 8, take exit 139 and turn right to the Renous Highway (Route 108), driving west toward Plaster Rock for roughly 26 km. At 46°49'55.8" N, 66°05'59.7" W, turn right onto the woods road known to the locals as Little Southwest Road. Drive another 26 km north to a camp road at 46°54'12.9" N, 66°24'12.3" W and drive approximately 350 m to 46°54'23.0" N, 66°24'07.7" W. Turn right and drive roughly 400 m and turn right again at 46°54'30.5" N, 66°23'51.7" W. Drive this rough road for about 1.6 km and turn left at 46°53'48.4" N, 66°23'09.9" W. Continue for 640 m to the trailhead and park, not blocking the camp road.

Trailhead: 46°53'44.5" N, 66°22'40.5" W **Waterfall:** 46°54'04.9" N, 66°20'36.3" W

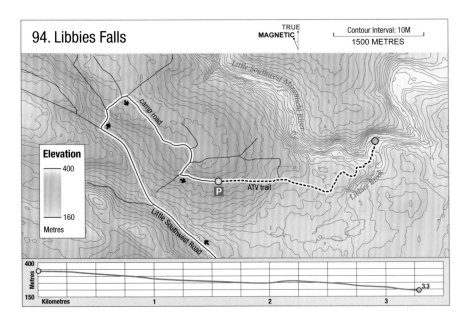

94. Libbies Falls (lower)

The hike: From the parking area, follow the well-used ATV trail straight ahead through a hardwood forest that is beautiful in autumn. Stay to the right on the main road until reaching a small clearing and take the ATV trail on the left. Follow the ridge that parallels Libbies Brook, and within minutes, the sound of falls can be heard.

Libbies Brook drains a myriad of small lakes and wetlands and runs relatively flat until it drops over a rocky outcrop, producing a tiered waterfall about 100 m before it joins the Little Southwest Miramichi River. There is a good vantage point near the top of the falls, as well as an excellent location at the bottom. Arriving at Libbies Falls is one of those moments when the natural beauty of this province takes your breath away. Old photographs show a "log slide" over the waterfall, a common practice during the heyday of lumbering in the 1800s to help logs glide through a constricted waterway.

94. Libbies Falls (upper)

95. Bartholomew River Falls

Type: Drop
Height: 3 m
Best season(s): Spring, fall
Access: Trail
Source: North Branch Bartholomew River
Distance (one way): 2.2 km
Difficulty: Easy to moderate

Rating: 3
Hiking time: 1 hour
Land ownership: Crown
Map: NTS 021J09 Doaktown
Nearby waterfall(s): Fall Brook Falls (York)
Cellphone coverage: N

Finding the trailhead: Head north from Fredericton to Doaktown on Route 8. Just beyond the bridge spanning the Southwest Miramichi River, turn left onto Hazelton Road. Head out this paved road approximately 6.7 km until it meets Dungarvon Road. This is the main hauling road for logging activities and can be pretty active with trucking. Turn left and drive roughly 10 km to the Y junction and stay right, continuing over the logging bridges on the South Branch Bartholomew River and the North Branch Bartholomew River. Turn left at 46°37'37.7" N, 66°19'33.0" W onto the road to King Brook. Resume driving for roughly 4 km to the trailhead on the left.

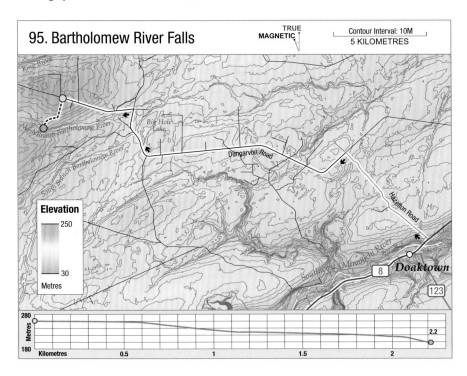

Trailhead: 46°37'57.2" N, 66°22'34.2" W   **Waterfall:** 46°37'5.6" N, 66°23'25.0" W

The hike: Hike the old logging road in a southerly direction down toward the river. This is a very enjoyable walk in the woods, but err on the side of caution as there is logging activity along this road. It is also frequented by ATVs heading to the falls. The area immediately next to the waterfall is a mix of coniferous trees. Just below the falls, look for a large burl on an eastern white cedar. From the main waterfall to the next rocky constriction roughly 100 m downriver, the riverbed contains jagged outcrops that would turn this section of river to turbulent waves in high water.

Bartholomew River Falls is an anomaly of sorts, located in the transition between two geologically different zones. At the falls, the river crosses an outcropping of the harder basalt rock of the Uplands ecoregion, then, for the majority of its length, it continues through predominantly sandstone bedrock within the low undulating hills of the New Brunswick Lowlands.

96. Fall Brook Falls (York)

Type: Drop
Height: 33 m
Best season(s): Summer, fall
Access: Trail
Source: Fall Brook (York)
Distance (one way): 742 m
Difficulty: Easy to moderate

Rating: 5
Hiking time: 40 minutes
Land ownership: Private (Irving Woodlands, fees apply)
Map: NTS 021J10 Hayesville
Nearby waterfall(s): Porter Brook Falls (Northumberland), Bartholomew River Falls
Cellphone coverage: N

Finding the trailhead: Head north from Fredericton to Boiestown on Route 8. Turn left onto Route 625 (Parker Ridge) and drive for nearly 4 km, staying right at the Y junction. Stay right again at Bloomfield Ridge Road and continue toward Holtville, crossing over the Southwest Miramichi River on what is known locally as the Norrad Bridge. Stay left at County Line Road until you come to the McKiel Gate, which is open from 6:00 a.m to 8:00 p.m. daily. Note that there is no entrance after 7:00 p.m. Contact the gatehouse at 506-365-0988 before heading out. Once you are there, the gatekeeper will allow passage through and give further directions to the falls after you have signed a waiver and paid a $10 access fee. Drive approximately 16 km to the access road on the left before the bridge and another 750 m on it to park at the top of the hill.

96. Fall Brook Falls (York)

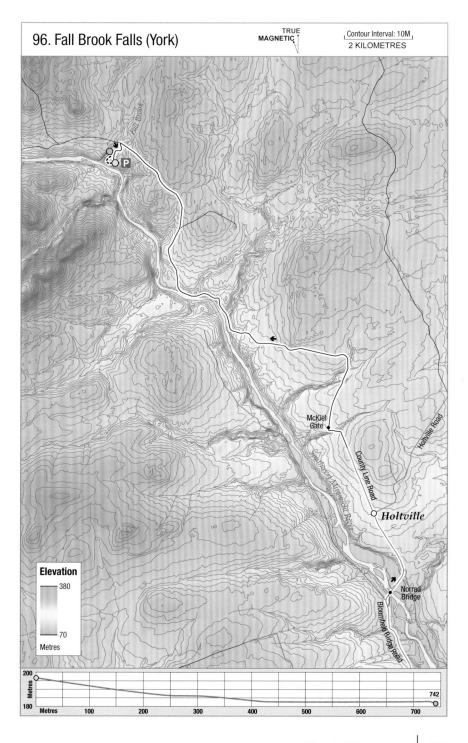

TRUE
MAGNETIC

Contour Interval: 10M
2 KILOMETRES

P

Fall Brook

McKiel
Gate

Holtville

Holtville Road

County Line Road

South West Miramichi River

Norrad
Bridge

Bloomfield Ridge Road

Elevation
380
70
Metres

200
Metres
180

Metres   100   200   300   400   500   600   700

742

Trailhead: 46°35'45.4" N, 66°35'19.2" W
Waterfall: 46°35'54.4" N, 66°35'24.4" W

The hike: Head down the woods road to the brook and a well-established trail leading to the falls. Due to the sheerness of the gorge, the trail has handrails and ropes to help you navigate around outcrops. Fall Brook Falls in York County is reputed to be one of the highest falls in New Brunswick, second only to the seasonal waterfall at Walton Glen Gorge. Although the brook is small, it is quite impressive where it drops more than 33 m.

This Fall Brook Falls has a commanding presence. The sound of thundering water reverberates in a natural amphitheatre, performing a symphony that drowns out other sounds along the path. Plumes of mist drift down the ravine, keeping the area moist and emerald green. If venturing here earlier in the year than June, be prepared to bushwhack around and over trees; the steepness of the ravine usually means that the snow can remain until then. However, the reward is well worth the effort at any time of the year.

Upon his first exploration of the falls in 1908, naturalist William Francis Ganong noted in his journal, "It is not truly vertical, but runs in a symmetrical sheet down the very steep face of a great cliff, against the ledges of which it is dashed to the finest veil of fleecy lace, while all the surroundings are strikingly wild and fine."

96. Fall Brook Falls (York)

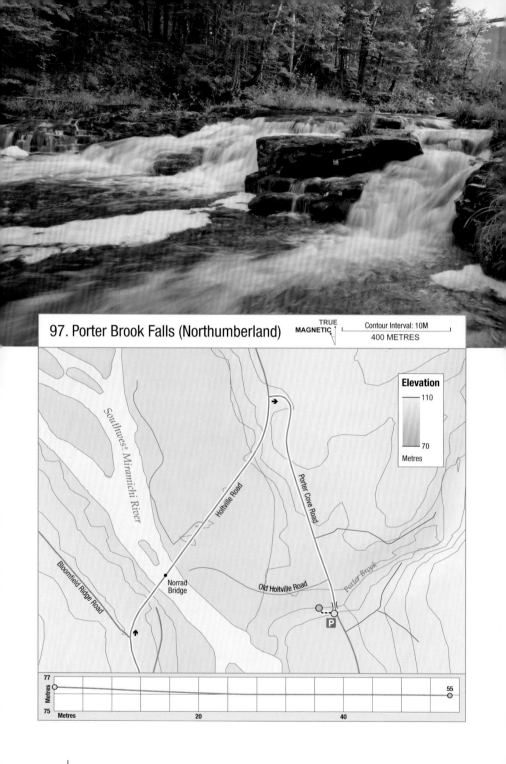

97. Porter Brook Falls (Northumberland)

TRUE
MAGNETIC

Contour Interval: 10M
400 METRES

Elevation
110
70
Metres

Southwest Miramichi River

Holtville Road

Porter Cove Road

Bloomfield Ridge Road

Norrad Bridge

Old Holtville Road

Porter Brook

P

77
Metres
75
55
Metres   20   40

97. Porter Brook Falls (Northumberland)

Type: Cascade
Height: 2 m
Best season(s): Spring, fall
Access: Trail
Source: Porter Brook (Northumberland)
Distance (one way): 55 m
Difficulty: Easy

Rating: 2
Hiking time: 5 minutes
Land ownership: Private
Map: NTS 021J10 Hayesville
Nearby waterfall(s): Fall Brook Falls
Cellphone coverage: Y

Finding the trailhead: Head north from Fredericton to Boiestown on Route 8. At Boiestown, turn left onto Route 625 (Parker Ridge) and drive for nearly 4 km, staying right at the Y junction. Stay right again on Bloomfield Ridge Road and continue toward Holtville, crossing over the Southwest Miramichi River on what is known locally as the Norrad Bridge. Just beyond the bridge, look for Porter Cove Road on the right. Turn here and drive roughly 860 m to the bridge over Porter Brook and park alongside the road.

Trailhead: 46°28'54.7" N, 66°28'24.9" W   **Waterfall:** 46°28'55.0" N, 66°28'27.4" W

The hike: From the roadside, hike down the access road that parallels the brook to the short path leading to the falls. The brook cascades over a series of ledges before entering the Southwest Miramichi River just below the Norrad Bridge. It is very picturesque, especially in autumn when the waterfall is draped in a cornucopia of colour.

Porter Brook flows through a mixed countryside of farms and forest, and this pristine brook is one of hundreds of ice-cold waters in the region that are home to the elusive Atlantic salmon. They are known to make their way up Porter Brook, climbing the rapids and falls to reach their spawning grounds further up the brook. This is salmon fishing country, so if there is someone fly fishing, be prepared to wait, or you can head to nearby Fall Brook Falls, one of the highest waterfalls in New Brunswick.

98. Chase Brook Falls

TRUE
MAGNETIC

Contour Interval: 10M
3 KILOMETRES

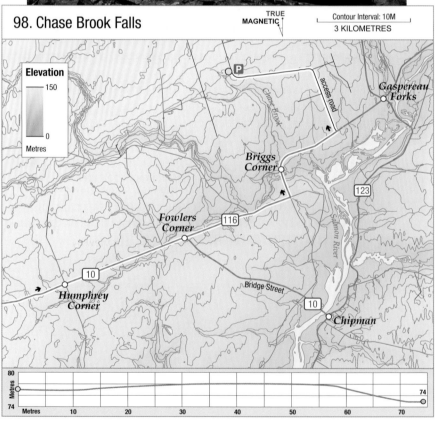

Elevation

150

0

Metres

P

Gaspereau Forks

Chase Brook

access road

Briggs Corner

123

Salmon River

Fowlers Corner

116

10

Bridge Street

Humphrey Corner

10

Chipman

80

Metres

74

74

Metres 10 20 30 40 50 60 70

98. Chase Brook Falls

Type: Drop
Height: 4 m
Best season(s): Spring, fall
Access: Trail
Source: Chase Brook
Distance (one way): 74 m
Difficulty: Easy

Rating: 2
Hiking time: 5 minutes
Land ownership: Crown
Map: NTS 021I04 Chipman
Nearby waterfall(s): Midland Falls
Cellphone coverage: Y

Finding the trailhead: From the village of Minto, drive toward Chipman on Route 10. Near Chipman, take Route 116 for Harcourt and drive to the intersection at Briggs Corner. Turn left and continue on toward Gaspereau Forks. The access road is along the north side of Route 116 at coordinates 46°13'44.1" N, 65°52'33.9" W. Drive out on the access road approximately 5 km to the trailhead on the left. The first 1.5 km is deeply rutted, but beyond this, it is a very good road.

Trailhead: 46°14'46.6" N, 65°55'08.8" W   **Waterfall:** 46°14'46.0" N, 65°55'12.1" W

The hike: The serene invitation of Chase Brook Falls can be heard from the trailhead. Follow an undefined trail into an open wooded area covered in a lush layer of pine needles to the sound of the waterfall. Near the top of the falls are a picnic table and a fire pit. There is a rope strung between trees to help with the descent down to the base of the falls.

Located within the New Brunswick Lowlands, an area with low undulating hills strewn with meadows and shallow ponds, the brook meanders innocently along until crashing over a ridge, formed by a change in geology, to make the falls. Similar to the Bartholomew River Falls, this waterfall seems out of place. A unique feature is a large rock partially blocking the water from view most of the year. During the spring freshet, the water velocity and volume push a waterfall over this rock, but the water drops down out of view by mid-summer. With time, the slow, unhurried erosive work of water and ice will trigger the boulder to fall outward, exposing the entire height of Chase Brook Falls.

99. Midland Falls

TRUE
MAGNETIC

Contour Interval: 10M
2 KILOMETRES

Elevation
90

10
Metres

Midland Rd

P

Perley Brook

10

Post Road

Salmon Bay

Cedar Street

Newcastle Creek

Main Street

Lake Drive

Pleasant Drive

Minto

23
Metres
18
Metres | 100 | 200

266

99. Midland Falls

Type: Cascade
Height: 3 m
Best season(s): Spring, summer, fall
Access: Trail
Source: Perley Brook
Distance (one way): 266 m
Difficulty: Easy

Rating: 1
Hiking time: 10 minutes
Land ownership: Private
Map: NTS 021I04 Chipman
Nearby waterfall(s): Chase Falls
Cellphone coverage: Y

Finding the trailhead: At the intersection of Main Street with Pleasant Drive (Route 10) in the village of Minto, drive north toward Chipman. Look for Post Road on the right about 1 km beyond the bridge over Newcastle Creek. Turn right and drive roughly 7.8 km out on Post Road to Midland Road on the left. Look for the pond on your left side, approximately 380 m along Midland Road. The trailhead and parking area are near the road just before the pond.

Trailhead: 46°08'02.9" N, 65°58'28.4" W **Waterfall:** 46°07'58.2" N, 65°58'38.2" W

The hike: Follow the road along the edge of the pond to the falls. The road is very slippery after it rains. Surrounded by poplar and birch trees, the waterfall has an unnatural facade; it appears to have been created as a result of strip-mining operations in the Minto and Chipman area. I am guessing that Perley Brook might have been diverted by nature, or by human intervention, after the area was open-pit mined along a coal seam. Regardless, the waterfall's man-made pond with its unusual, almost baby-blue tint, stretches from the base of the falls to Midland Road. The bedrock at the falls is reddish in colour, probably due to trace iron deposits, and oddly enough, the brook flows eastward into Grand Lake at Iron Bound Cove.

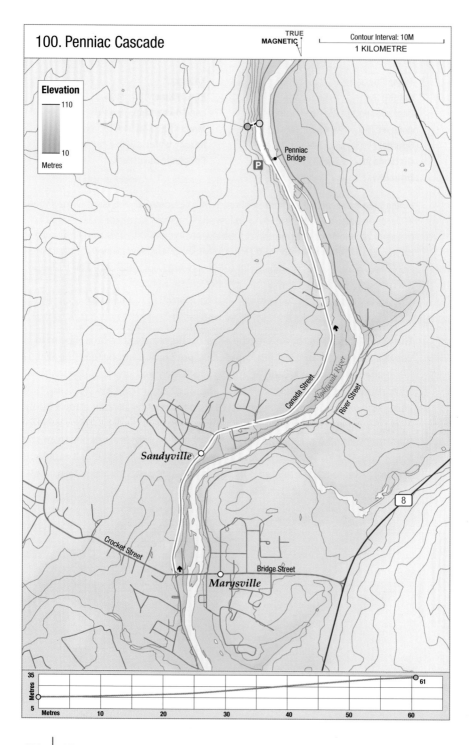

100. Penniac Cascade

TRUE
MAGNETIC

Contour Interval: 10M
1 KILOMETRE

Elevation

110

10

Metres

Penniac
Bridge

P

Sandyville

Canada Street

Nashwaak River

River Street

8

Crocket Street

Bridge Street

Marysville

35
Metres
5

Metres   10   20   30   40   50   60

61

100. Penniac Cascade

Type: Cascade
Height: Various
Best season(s): Spring, fall
Access: Road, bushwhack
Source: Unidentified
Distance (one way): 61 m
Difficulty: Moderate

Rating: 1
Hiking time: 10 minutes
Land ownership: Private
Map: NTS 021J03 Burtts Corner
Nearby waterfall(s): N/A
Cellphone coverage: Y

Finding the trailhead: Within minutes of Fredericton, the Penniac Cascade is a great example of a roadside waterfall attraction. From the four-way intersection at the bridge in Marysville, drive north on Canada Street, following the west side of the Nashwaak River to Penniac Bridge. At the bridge, turn and park downriver 20 m or so from the bridge. This is a busy road, so please be aware of the traffic.

Trailhead: 46°00'30.4" N, 66°34'58.6" W
Waterfall: 46°00'40.1" N, 66°35'05.5" W

The hike: From the parking area, walk north along the highway to the brook. The designated coordinates will lead to one of the better locations to photograph the cascade. If further exploration is warranted, continue up the hill to where it begins to plateau. There are several good photographic opportunities. This seasonal waterfall has cut a passage to the Nashwaak River and is best viewed and photographed during the spring freshet or a few days after a heavy rain in autumn. The brook has no permanent source, such as a lake or wetland, to maintain its viability during the summer.

Acknowledgements

My intention on this return journey was to involve waterfall enthusiasts, friends, and family. To that end, I solicited information and support from enthusiasts Irving Peter-Paul and Cathy Doucet, who provided information on waterfalls in Westmorland and Kent Counties. Allain Pelletier contributed information on Madawaska County. Childhood friends Danny Harquail and Michael Levesque of Dalhousie joined me in the successful – and sometimes unsuccessful – search for waterfalls in Restigouche County. Our unsuccessful quest for three waterfalls at the head of the South Charlo River will always remain one of my highlights. After a long, tiring, and very wet day of bushwhacking, it was decided those falls would have to wait for another time.

Another memorable adventure was with Stephane Patenaude, who drove me to Whites Brook Falls and Falls Brook Falls, a couple of his favourite waterfalls in the Restigouche River area. Ken Ramey Jr. also answered the call to join me, and he educated me on flora during our excursion to Bartholomew River Falls. My friend Rod O'Connell of Nigadoo provided tons of information about the Nepisiguit Mi'gmaq Trail and led me to a few unknown gems in Gloucester and Northumberland Counties. Jason Grant, of Pabineau First Nation, provided information on the etymology of Nepisguit. Lee Dickison of Meductic spent an evening with me, locating Sullivan Creek Falls.

My son Liam joined me on a few excursions as well, in particular to Parlee Brook Falls. Brother-in-law Larry McKay found time to visit three waterfalls. Terry Fearon and Brian Mercier spent an autumn afternoon looking for Roger Brook Falls and Sandburn Brook Falls. I want to acknowledge my good friend Terry Gallant of Turtle Creek, who gave graciously of his time, resources, and enthusiasm. Over the past ten years, Terry and I have located and photographed more than one hundred waterfalls together, many of which are in this new guide. Finally, and most importantly, I would be remiss if I left out my editor Alison Hughes, who kept it all in order and together.

Thank you all.

References

Bailey, L.W. *Report on the Mines and Minerals of New Brunswick: With an Account of the Present Condition of Mining Operations in the Province.* Fredericton: G.E. Fenety, 1864.

Eiselt, Marianne and H.A. *Hiking Trails of New Brunswick, 4th Edition.* Fredericton: Goose Lane Editions, 2018.

Guitard, Nicholas. *The Lost Wilderness: Rediscovering W.F. Ganong's New Brunswick.* Fredericton: Goose Lane Editions, 2015.

——. *Waterfalls of New Brunswick: A Guide.* Fredericton: Goose Lane Editions, 2010.

Natural Resources Canada. n.d. "Atlas of Canada." Accessed September 24, 2020. https://www.atlas.gc.ca>toporama.

Natural Resources Canada. n.d. "Canadian Geographical Names Database." Accessed September 20, 2020. https://www.nrcan.gc.ca/earth-sciences/geography/querying-canadian-geographical-names-database/9170.

New Brunswick Department of Transportation. n.d. "Designated Highways." Accessed September 15, 2020. https://www.gnb.ca/0113/maps/mapbooks/2012-Mapbooks-e.asp

New Brunswick Natural Resources and Energy Development. n.d. Accessed September 24, 2020. https://www2.gnb.ca/content/gnb/en/departments/erd.html

New Brunswick Museum. n.d. "William Francis Ganong Correspondence S 217 F 3." *W.F. Ganong fonds, correspondence.*

Oromocto River Watershed Association. n.d. Accessed September 24, 2020. https://www.oromoctowatershed.ca.

Provincial Archives of New Brunswick. n.d. "Place Names of New Brunswick." Accessed September 24, 2020. https://archives.gnb.ca/Exhibits/Communities/Home.aspx?culture=en-CA.

Waterfalls of New Brunswick Facebook Group. n.d. https://www.facebook.com/WaterfallsNewBrunswick.

Nicholas Guitard is a photographer, canoeist, hiker, and engineer. Guitard's interest in waterfalls began in earnest when he attempted to find the falls at the Walton Glen Gorge near the Bay of Fundy and discovered there was little information to help hikers. He began collecting information on his website, waterfalls-new-brunswick.ca, and eventually released a photographic guide to New Brunswick's waterfalls and the first edition of *Waterfalls of New Brunswick: A Guide*.

In addition to his work chronicling New Brunswick's waterfalls, Guitard is also the author of *The Lost Wilderness*, an examination of the wilderness journeys of the naturalist W.F. Ganong, and a finalist for the New Brunswick Book Award for Nonfiction. Originally from the northern New Brunswick town of Dalhousie, Guitard now lives in Fredericton.